Leadership Fusion

Best Practices to Lead and Influence

Darcy Bien
Misty Bruns
Andy Foerster
Karla Lewis
Angela Rakis
Lacy Starling
Cyndi Wineinger

Melanie Booher
Katie Currens
Simcha Kackley
Barbara McMahan
Mike Sipple, Jr.
Joi Turner
Jodi Brandstetter

Influence Network Media

Copyright @ 2022 Influence Network Media

All Rights Reserved. Apart from any fair dealing for purposes of research or private study, or criticism or review, as permitted under the Copyright, Designs and Patents Act 1988, this publication may only be reproduced, stored or transmitted, in any form or by any means, with the prior permission in writing of the copyright owner, or in the case of the reprographic reproduction in accordance with the terms of licenses issued by the Copyright Licensing Agency. Enquires concerning reproduction outside those terms should be sent to the publisher.

Contents

	Foreword	vii
	Introduction	1
1.	Leadership Simplified	19
	Misty Bruns	33
2.	Inclusive Leadership	35
	Joi Turner	45
3.	Leading with Intention	47
	Mike Sipple Jr.	65
4.	Your Employees are Not Your Friends	69
	Lacy Starling	81
5.	What Kind Of Leader Are You?	85
	Karla Lewis	99
6.	ABCs of Organizational Purpose	101
	Katie Currens	119
7.	Breathe Before You Lead	123
	Barbara McMahan	141
8.	The Practice of Organizational Leadership	143
	Andy Foerster	167
9.	Strategy in Motion	171
	Darcy Bien	199
10.	The Growth Culture	203

	Cyndi Wineinger	229
11.	A Legacy Worth Remembering	233
	Melanie Booher	253
12.	The Role of the CRO	257
	Angela Rakis	271
13.	Sales Enablement	273
	Simcha Kackley	303
	Conclusion	307
	About the Publisher	309
	Business Fusion Book Series	311
	Book Smarts Business Podcast	313

Foreword

Inspiring the Next Evolution of Work

The world of work was already evolving prior to COVID-19 impacts, but it was this universal, global push to work from home that effectively led to everyone stopping their work habits at that time. It also created the opportunity for everyone to re-enter the workplace with a clean slate, approaching work with a fresh mindset. This book comes at a timely point in the evolution of the global workforce and how we approach leadership and talent management and develop new processes for effective and efficient work practices.

What's the problem?

We live in a data-driven, socially-overloaded, fast-paced global society that expects businesses to support the development of products and processes that address needs while also creating and supporting the vision of the future. Not only are outcome expectations changing, but worker-needs and requirements are changing, too. Work has become more than just something one does as a means to an end; it is a meaningful endeavor that helps define who we are, an extension of life that increases expectations for flexibility, even oftentimes over money. It also means individuals are no longer focused on staying with a job or company for their entire career but rather using moves between companies to support personal growth, upskilling, and cultivation of meta-expertise across multiple areas of focus to drive vertical achievement. Finally, COVID-19 forced nearly all workers to change a significant portion of their processes, particularly the requirement to work from home. This was an enormous change from working face-to-face, together, to working solo within a distributed team.

With so many changes happening all at once, they signal the need for a full procedural, structural change that drives a review of leadership focus and techniques, talent identification, management, and development, and workforce processes and structure.

What are we doing now?

Until 2020, we were operating in the 21st century; using leftover industrialized processes and goals to create outcomes that would have been more successful in the last century. Much like education, it is necessary to evolve every aspect of workforce development, management, and leadership to ensure employees are empowered to design and deliver work that will be competitive in this century; where creativity, personalization, and precise, data-driven outcomes are valued over industrialized, efficiency-focused goals.

Workdays to date have followed a traditional time-based model of 40 hours per week, eight hours per day, and five days per week. Yet, many work far more than those hours, some of which are filled with unnecessary tasks to justify the pay. In other words, rather than capitalizing on the best individual work hours and talent-driven outcomes, success is too often defined by the amount of time spent working. Consequently, workers are cogs in a wheel; they are hired to do a task rather than being hired for growth capability, creativity, and work products. Lastly, hierarchical leadership based on time in service follows a similar thought process. Workers are not more or less capable because they have a certain number of years of experience or age. This concept, again, assumes that as experience grows, so too does expertise; but with a constantly evolving consumer environment, new capabilities and a creative mind are often needed and can even add fresh innovative thinking to a space that would otherwise continue in a linear, assembly-line fashion to develop the ever-similar widgets.

What do we need?

To progress forward, vision, strategy, and innovation are needed to help evolve and inspire the workforce of the future. Workers will need to learn continuously to ensure upskilling is a constant, rather than momentary, focus; like in graduate school. Badges and certificates should become more and more common as shorter, more specific learning needs are met more frequently. Personalized working conditions, processes, and trajectories will not only better meet the needs of workers but also allow companies to capitalize on their talents, unique abilities, and experiences in a way that was eliminated previously by the system's structure. Finally, with a large portion of workers now working from home – or anywhere, really –

the need to share energy and ideas and to especially keep an inspired workforce is expected to expand exponentially.

How do we get there?

Leadership, management, and process ideas must evolve to focus on the ultimate goal of, not so much efficiency, but more so effectiveness. Inspired workers who can capitalize on their personal skills, experiences, and capabilities will naturally work efficiency into the system because fewer resources will be wasted on time-driven activities and measurements. Instead of focusing on extraneous work actions based on old metrics and expectations, time will be spent on targeting outcome-based actions, and success will be measured by production over time. Truly, the days of punching a timeclock need to be of the past. Leadership and management will fixate less on controlling an assembly line of workers and activities and more on inspiring emotions and ideas, balancing mental and physical health, promoting teamwork and expertise development, and hiring for growth over tasking alone.

Leadership

Looking back over the past 100 years, the focus of leadership has been to define goals, project actions, and assign tasks; often with a single, or small, group of leaders. Today, leadership can be more democratized, with many levels, types, and people from different backgrounds making decisions, driving innovation, and helping create vision. Areas of focus have also changed alongside leadership, requiring inspiring the workforce, energizing people, and having to answer the challenge of creating personal meaning for each team member. People don't just want a job anymore; they want one that is meaningful and impactful to the world.

In this book, we highlight how to "Breathe Before You Lead" (McMahan, chapter 7), showing how to recognize the need to be centered in order to help guide your workforce to maximize their cognitive capabilities, creative ideas, and mental health. "What Kind of Leader are You?" (Lewis, chapter 5) will walk the reader through a personal review and assessment to support becoming a better servant leader who understands the team and doesn't take shortcuts. "Inclusive Leadership" (Turner, chapter 2) will help shape processes and thinking to increase the inclusion of all backgrounds, ideas, experiences, and differences among teams to maximize success. None of this will be as impactful as it can be unless one is "Leading with Intention" (Sipple, chapter 3). This chapter will focus on techniques, such as active listening, gratitude, and how to utilize real-time feedback to help workers thrive in the current high-paced environment. Finally, "Leadership Simplified" (Misty Bruns, chapter 1) takes a straightforward look at how all these capabilities can be organized into a clear, easy-to-follow, and repeatable process that will help even the most experienced leaders innovate into the future.

Talent Management

Talent management has evolved substantially over the past 30 years as the workforce has progressed from an industrial model to a fluid, dynamic, personalized ecosystem of talent that no longer stays with one company; instead of migrating through several over the lifetime. Management has also broadened to include identification, development, and supervision, in addition to recognizing the benefits of diversity in bringing different experiences, belief systems, cultural knowledge, and varying expertise to increase creative success. To identify better talent, competencies rather than degrees are becoming the focus of many employers, and for continuous learning, credentials and badges are allowing for lifelong learning opportunities.

In this book, several chapters will help guide the development of insights and building skills in talent management. "Your Employees are Not Your Friends" (Starling, chapter 4) will help you understand how to get to know everyone in your organization while also maintaining an appropriate and professional distance between you and their circles. "The Growth Culture" (Wineinger, chapter 10) will provide direction on how to develop talent and keep the workforce active in their own learning and growth, as well as for serving company needs (Simcha Kackley, chapter 13). "Sales Enablement" (Kackley, chapter 13) will also define and clarify how to maintain a workforce growth environment and develop a growth mindset for critical thinking and development.

Processes

A significant amount of attention, though, has been on developing new processes since the global workforce went home for public health reasons due to the global COVID-19 pandemic. After nearly two years of generous work-from-home plans, the workforce has effectively undone a sizable number of historically common practices, now allowing for a full redesign of how work is organized and expected to occur. This complete shutdown of nearly all traditional practices for this length of time has allowed for the potential reconstruction of work, leading to hybrid conditions and significantly more flexibility. Yet the questions that remain to be answered are: "How do we plan forward, and what is the optimal balance of working from home, office, or elsewhere? What flexibility of time works best?"

This book will highlight several of the key elements needed to improve processes across the workforce. The first step to address is how to strategically do this. "Strategy in Motion" (Bien, chapter 9) will help clarify what organizations want to achieve and the how-to steps for achieving those goals. "The Practice of Organizational Leadership" (Foerster, chapter 8) will build upon this vision to clarify and define how to not only optimize the efficiency of the workforce but also lead with purpose. Purposeful leadership is not the only focus, though. Purposeful and meaningful work is important, too; these concepts are highlighted in the "ABCs of Organizational Purpose." (Katie Currens, chapter 6) It's no longer about work-life balance; instead, it's about work-life integration, and with that comes the expectation that work is an extension of our views, values, and selves. We strive for deeper meaning from the work we do, and so it is the job of every leader to align behaviors, opportunities, and tasking to support the organization and the individuals within it. Ultimately, all of these efforts are intended to support sales and movement of products or services, making "The Role of the CRO" a necessary component of ensuring the organization is moving in the right direction (Rakis, chapter 12).

Why will this work better?

Designing a fully formed plan for improved working conditions, leadership, and management must begin with the end in mind. Applying the principles of human-centered design allows us to think about what the optimal working conditions look like and work backward from that vision. Each of the chapters included in *Leadership Fusion* will walk the reader through this extended process to achieve the goals of each organization. Living plans will also be necessary and will support the continuous evolution that will be needed (e.g., personalization, continuous learning) to, not only capitalize on the talents of each individual but also create the stability and longevity achieved only by flexible organizations that can adjust to every new challenge. Lastly, the greatest change will need to be made in the transition from an industrialized view of work to one that supports workers, not one that treats them like cogs in a wheel. We must take advantage of individual skills rather than reducing every person to a predetermined set of tasks.

Ultimately, success looks like a living ecosystem of ideas generated by workers inspired to create, explore, innovate, and drive successful outcomes.

Dr. J.J. Walcutt, scientist, innovator, learning engineer

Dr. J.J. Walcutt is a scientist, innovator, and learning engineer that specializes in strategic development and reform across education, military, and government. Dr. Walcutt is an industry leader in designing workforce structures and processes across both the public and private sectors. She previously served as a Human Innovation Fellow under the Office of Personnel Management, where she led the design efforts to create an open innovation model for re-imagining the executive branch. Her current work focuses on optimizing human cognition and performance across a wide spectrum of learning programs, including neuro-informed military training, data-driven higher education planning, and talent development optimization. Dr. Walcutt currently works with the Association for Talent Development to help further these goals for preparing our workforce for the future.

Introduction

Welcome to Leadership Fusion

I traveled across the country to present to a large organization's top leaders. This was an impressive team, brought in from states all over the US. The best of the best. A group of women who were known to be high-achievers and at the top of their game. Winners of all the awards. The top dogs who run their own independent agencies for the #1 personal insurance company in the US.

My mission was simple (and tied to my life's passion!) – to motivate these leaders to attract and retain top talent, improve their agency culture, and guide them towards a plan of inspiration and engagement for their teams. All of this which we know leads to success (great culture and profit!). Most often, leaders think they are creating a strong culture yet fail to put in the intentional planning to make it happen. Ask any leader if he/she operates without a Financial, Marketing, or Strategic plan – and you will get a resounding – "No way!" Nearly 100% of CEOs have those plans. Yet our studies show that less than 10% of leaders have a plan for People/Culture (even though they state that People/Culture are highly important to drive the bottom line for the organization). There's a big gap here that must be addressed. That's where my culture plan (the THRIVE Model^{TM})

comes into play! My company, PEOPLEfirst Talent & Retention has made it our mission to grow the elite 10% of leaders. We focus on the 90% who think they are addressing culture, but are not intentional in their plan. They "trust their guts" but fail to have a concrete plan. We help leaders develop a plan for People/Culture and ensure that plan is brought to life through visibility and habits.

Back to the big event. There were some administrative hoops to jump through beforehand, including our proposal/agreement – which outlined my responsibility as a speaker, the benefits of working with a culture coach, provided details on travel expenses, meals (which were to be reimbursed), and included attending one dinner with the participants to be available to informally chat with them outside of the speaking engagement. There was an itinerary that showed our Welcome Dinner on Sunday at 6:30 p.m. – and so I adjusted my travel plans to arrive Sunday afternoon to ensure my attendance without any flight/travel issues.

Additionally, the company required that I sign a "confidentiality agreement" which forbids me from mentioning the organization's name in any capacity. Not just related to posting on social media but not mentioning their name as my client in any capacity. I had asked if I could tell my spouse or parents, thinking if it wasn't related to social media – it should be fine. Nope, not even to my spouse or parents. I was approved to say "the #1 personal insurance company". Interesting. A literal gag order. While I'd never had something like this requested of me, I chalked it up to the unfortunate red tape of big corporations – and obliged because I desired to obtain the business and hoped for additional work down the road. These administrative details may seem unimportant right now, but they set the stage for what was about to occur during my trip.

Obtaining transportation to/from the resort and airport seemed a bit clunky. It's important to note that I am a planner. I try to prepare in advance for things and generally like to know how things will unfold (especially on a business trip where I am the guest speaker and timeliness is critically important). I had intentionally worked with the company representative to book my arrival the night before my speaking event. Mainly, I wanted to ensure that I was present and ready to go when they needed me the next morning. I also find it quite stressful to "wing it" in unknown circumstances (ex. in a city that I have never been to before!). What I did know is that the resort was about one hour outside of a big metropolitan area. No bus, train, or shuttle access. During our planning stages, I suggested a rental car, one planner recommended trying Uber, and the other planner suggested that I ride with one of the attendees who was flying in around the same time as me. Great, I had a partner to travel with to the resort and could potentially save the client some travel expenses. Sounded like a good plan to me!

Of course, that plan didn't last. The evening before the trip (transportation plans had been in place for over a month!) my partner had a last-minute flight change outside of her control and I found myself without a plan for transportation. My would-be travel partner recommended that I book a private car for myself and provided the information. Immediately I was nervous about the cost of a private car. Would the client still cover the cost or get angry with me for booking my own? (It was $163 each way which included a 20% tip...could I have obtained a rental car for a better price? What would an Uber cost to get to the destination? So many questions but no time for research given that my flight was the next day!)

So, I took her advice, and at 10:30 p.m. the night before my trip, I jumped on the phone to book my private car transportation. At this point, having a plan meant more to me than having financial approval. I was willing to pay extra – myself if needed – to ensure that I would arrive on time and safely at the resort. I figured that my would-be travel partner was taking her car by herself and trusted her knowledge of how the organization handled things like this.

Sunday went by in a blur. In the morning, I finished packing my bags and told my husband about the family plans as I departed for the airport. He encourage me: "You got this babe – we have a combination of carpools to cover two soccer games, the lacrosse game for the girls, a friend will take our son to/from a birthday party and I had a sub arranged for bowling league." His eyes widened in annoyance. Alas…it was all planned out and mama was headed to the airport! It takes a ton of planning, but with a tribe of helpers in my stead, I was certain that all would be okay. I knew my hubby could handle things without me for two days. (More like one and a half but who was counting?!)

The flight was fine and I had a text from my driver when I landed telling me where to meet them. It was a huge relief to my travel anxiety to see that text come through. My first time having a private car was falling into place all as it should. The driver opened the door for me, handled my baggage, helped me into the decked-out black Suburban, offered me drinks, and welcomed me to his city. It was much a more opulent experience than this suburban mom is used to.

My mind wandered as I envisioned all of the attendees booking their own private cars and driver to arrive at a fancy resort. I thought to myself "Is this how elite leaders handle transportation when they travel? Was I going to annoy my expense report approver because I got a car like the other attendee? Could I have saved money by renting a car or getting an Uber?" I thought about how I could work this situation into my presentation the next day. Communication gaps, attention to detail, setting expectations for others, and helping them through uncertainty. Ahh...so many thoughts were swirling around my head.

As we drove from the airport to the resort – my thoughts shifted as I took in the beautiful landscape and listened to lovely elevator music playing in my decked-out ride. We made our way through beautiful, rolling, green hills and pulled into the winding drive of the resort. As the building came into view, I stared in absolute amazement. It was simply gorgeous. It was definitely the finest resort that I had ever seen.

The driver again opened my door and helped me with luggage, while the bellhop came to offer assistance. Once I was checked in, I went up to my room. It was beautiful as well. As I unpacked, someone knocked on the door. It was a resort employee, bringing me a plate of chocolate-covered strawberries and welcoming me to the resort. It was impressive customer relations and definitely made me feel special.

I reviewed the itinerary for the next couple of days and checked to make sure I was making good time. No flight delays, no snowstorms. So far so good. The "Welcome Itinerary" showed a dinner onsite at the resort starting at 6:30 p.m. I freshened up my make-up a bit and slipped on some nicer shoes (yeah, I was wearing my favorite slip-on tennis shoes for travel). Then I made my way downstairs.

I had a hard time finding the restaurant, and of course, didn't know any of the faces that would attend this event. That's always an awkward situation. When I saw another lady also looking around seeming a bit confused like myself, I guessed that we might be in the same boat (looking for a hard-to-find restaurant to meet up with a group of female leaders). I attempted to engage with her and asked: "Hi, I noticed you are looking for someone. Any chance you are also looking for the on-site Restaurant?" She looked at me in a strangely puzzled manner, and quickly said, "No." That was it. No nice-ities. No smile. No small talk. No offer to help. NOTHING. She turned on her heels and walked the other way. Obviously, this woman wasn't going to be in the tribe of culture-achievers that I was looking for – those who really care about people.

When I did find the right place, I was the first to arrive. It was 6:25 p.m. and, as I said I was the first to arrive, so I was the only one present. I said hello to the bartenders and wait staff who were ready and eagerly awaiting the group's arrival. I sheepishly asked for water, not wanting to start the party before the rest of the culture-group arrived. When I glanced at the table and saw thirteen lovely place settings (six on one side of the table and seven on the other). The three-course menu card was nicely placed on each plate, with silverware, and fancy wine glasses.

I mingled a bit with the waitstaff. 6:37 p.m. Still no one...

When they finally arrived, they were chatting and laughing with each other. They were, obviously, a group that had known each other for quite some time and enjoyed each other's company immensely. In fact, they enjoyed each other so much, that those around them seemed to fade into the walls with little/no recognition. I glanced at the faces around me to see if any seemed familiar. As I perused the room, the only familiar face was the unhelpful woman from the bar. Great...I guess she was part of this group after all. A thought crossed my mind: I hold successful leaders to a higher standard of understanding people and possessing skills to relate to others. This woman might have found the restaurant/people she was also seeking – but based on our brief interaction, she had some additional self-finding that needed to occur to make her a better leader. Recognizing that human moments and interactions with others matter. All of them. Not just those within peer groups. But those with subordinates (teammates!) and strangers, too. Those outside our normal social network. Again my mind was working...I put this thought aside to revisit later and discover a tactful way to work a lesson into my presentation for the next day...

Upon gingerly meandering into a few discussions, I introduced myself to several ladies. Good news, I was greeted warmly, "Oh yes, Melanie – you are with us! Join us!" But something was amiss. I could feel inquisitive stares from some of the ladies. as I was the obvious outsider that didn't quite fit in with this group and who knew each other so well.

And then it hit me...I wasn't invited to this dinner. The itinerary did not state who exactly was to be in attendance, and apparently, the welcome dinner only included their internal team. It was not for the speaker who traveled across the country to speak with them and build into them at the next day's event. As I processed these new thoughts, my mind continued to race. I wanted to see how they handled an uncomfortable situation like this. Because there are a few ways to handle errors like this:

1. With grace and compassion
2. With awkward uncertainty
3. With indignant disdain

The two ladies who planned the event stopped their chit-chat and meandered toward me. One of them was so uncomfortable that she avoided eye contact. She quickly said hello and scurried off again leaving the other lady to bask in and deal with the discomfort. And that's putting it lightly. The interaction varied between two to three from above. Awkward at best...downright dismissive and snobby at worst. My host counted the seats and counted those in attendance a few times. As if thirteen was so large a number that it's difficult to account for?

Now, personally, I love watching and assessing these kinds of human moments. Witnessing and learning from the ways that people deal with situations in times like this. Does the person rise to the occasion or succumb to the awkwardness? In this case, definitely the latter.

I asked if she cared that I joined the group for dinner (I mean, after all, they were paying for my dinner either way, as written into our travel agreement). She could barely make a sentence. Her body language told the tale of discomfort. Her words quivered a bit. "It's just...well...(counting seats again, counting people again)..." And all too quickly, I let the squirming fish off the hook. Maybe I should have waited longer, but I did the humane thing and put her out of her misery.

"Hey, don't worry about it. I can walk over there and go eat at the bar." (Which was just down the hall). I could feel the growing number of stares from the group as people watched this moment of social discomfort unfold. The two planners were very uncomfortable, to say the least. Their gut reaction did not include a resolution that was a win/win solution.

Stop and think about this moment. If you were a leader in this situation, what might have been a better way to handle it? In my world, it's called radical candor (show you care, and speak directly) with a lean-in toward inclusivity. It would not have taken much extra effort to say, "Grab a beverage and let's pull up another seat!" That is how, I believe, emotionally intelligent leaders would have handled this unnecessarily uncomfortable social encounter. After all, remember that there were six seats on one side and seven on the other. They could've easily pulled up a spot for one extra person.

I laughed it off and went on to eat dinner in the bar by myself. It was an amazing meal. I made some friends with two ladies sitting next to me and the server who made light conversation and laughed at my situation. They agreed that it was strange that the guest speaker wasn't included in the welcome dinner.

When my new dinner friends departed, we said our goodbyes. I glanced down at their table and noticed that one of them had accidentally forgotten her cell phone. Split-second decision:

1. Do I let the server handle it and hold it as lost and found, hoping that the ladies return before getting too far away or
2. Dash out the door like a madwoman and chase them into the parking lot with hopes they have not made it too far?

I went with choice B. I grabbed it and bolted out the door.

Luckily, I found them walking down the hallway. They were very thankful for my quick reaction, and also found it very funny that I looked like a thief who was skipping out on their dinner bill! Oops! I hoped that the server and wait staff didn't assume the worst. Good news, I returned to the bar and no one even realized I was gone.

When I got back to my room, I had a moment to think about how things had unfolded throughout the evening. While my group dinner didn't work out as planned, I had made the best of it – and I'd made some new friends in the process. I had handled the awkward situation with grace, let the planner off the hook for her error, made new friends, and run out the door to save the day with the found cell phone – all good things. I figured that good karma should follow. But I also wasn't about to allow the night to pass without a lesson surfacing. My mind was racing. For myself and those who experienced it with me – and who I would be speaking to the next day!

During my bedtime check-in call to say good night to my family, my husband and I chatted about some of the evening's events. We deliberated on how I could utilize what had occurred and reapply it to the presentation the next day. Remember, I was going to be motivating these high-end power leaders about creating a strong culture within their own agency. Helping them attract and retain top talent, improve their agency culture, and guide them towards a plan of inspiration and engagement of their teams. All of this is in order to drive success and help them thrive. Based on what I had experienced, if their teams were feeling any of the things I had experienced (poor communication, lack of planning, non-inclusive group dynamics, etc.) – there were definite areas for improvement.

Now, it was my task to just help them see those opportunities for themselves. I had to do it in a way that opened the door for self-reflection, without attacking anyone or making them feel terrible about the prior night's incident. All in a manner that spoke to the human side of their business mind. There were so many lessons wrapped in one event.

First, organizational culture shows its true colors in the behaviors that replicate when no one is looking. It's all about how you treat others in the toughest of times. As a leader, what behaviors do you desire from your team? Are they aligned with your brand? Do people make the best of challenging situations?

In hindsight, when a big national organization requests that you NOT use their name, trust that there's a reason behind it. Probably not a good one. The higher ups in that organization know that there is some serious work that needs to be done. (And if any of them are reading this now – I challenge you to step up to the plate and make some changes! When we know better, we do better. Hold yourself to a higher standard. Lead with heart. Treat others with respect.)

Do they feel empowered to make changes to things that are already set in motion? Or do they stay the path because "that's how it's always been done"? Taking some risk is needed. It's important to note that these leaders are literally in the business of risk. They monetize how we pay for the risks that we take in life. Yet both of the planners of the dinner didn't feel comfortable thinking outside the box to resolve any potential areas of growth. They weren't comfortable with doing things a little differently or changing the game mid-stream. It may not have been what they originally planned, but flexing (bend and don't break!) is necessary. Change the way things have been done in the past.

Additionally, leaders within large organizations always need to be willing to put themselves in others' shoes. Going back to my leadership presentation story from before: how would you have wanted to be treated if you were the person not invited to dinner? How would you have wanted them to handle the situation once the mistake had been recognized? When you are in the group that's included, sometimes it's hard to think how someone that is excluded may feel. Why not have a "the more the merrier" attitude? If we spent more time thinking of others' feelings, first and foremost, a situation like the one I found myself in would have gone down very differently.

Leadership Lessons

This story is just one of many that brings to light the challenges that come with being a good and effective leader. A simple itinerary miscommunication and the awkwardness of not knowing how to react to something differently. It takes courage to lead the change. Leadership. Change leadership.

So now we must ask ourselves, what truly makes a great leader? Over the years, I've worked with some impressive people – a variety of leaders with varying styles, experience, and certainly notions for motivating others. That's the glory of being a leader – we can each lead in our own, unique way.

Does everyone believe that they are a good leader? Or do they truly understand that they might make a better follower? Are there certain styles of leadership that are easier to follow than others? What makes a leader rise to the top? Even if they are someone whose leadership style is less about leading and more about ruling? (I'm thinking of the Adolph Hitler types here...)

I enjoy leading. Whether on a sports team, school club, sorority, neighborhood gathering, board membership, corporate team, family related or entrepreneurial teams – you name it – I've pretty much led through it. As an example, it never bothered me to wear a "We Be Drug-Free" shirt in high school, when peer pressure is at its highest and others surely thought I was a big nerd. To this day, my friend Randy still likes to poke fun at those damn shirts. It's been a running joke since high school. And yet the lesson in wearing the shirt with my team was huge.

Our team knew the importance of making good decisions and leading with conviction of those decisions, regardless of what others said about the shirt/us. It was an easier thing to do, because we did it together. Lead the way, and others will follow. However, there are many who would have folded under that peer pressure. (Who uses that language anyway..."We Be Drug-Free." It's quirky and rhymes but it's not a teenager's dream to wear this! In fact it might actually be more of a nightmare...but I digress...)

What is strong leadership?

When I stop to think about the essence of strong leadership, experiential stories like the one above, and other life lessons, begin to bubble to the surface. I have definitely learned from some of the best and some of the worst, emulating the good things and leaving the bad behind.

In different stages of life, we encounter opportunities to hone our leadership skills. In retrospect, some of the biggest life lessons have arisen out of rather negative situations under bad leaders. Those tend to stand out as the biggest lessons and opportunities for improvement.

What if everyone took the time to reflect upon those negative situations and learn from the most challenging situations in our lives? Often our gut reaction is to just get through and bury it in our past – but those painful moments can often reveal some amazing lessons if we take the time to dissect and learn from them!

Pondering on those moments can prove to be useful in molding us into great leaders. Helping us on both a personal and professional front. Here are some of the takeaways that I've been given based on some of those challenging moments:

- Lead with integrity and don't do things behind others backs. Operate from a place of abundance (not just when it serves your purpose, but even in the challenging moments!) to lift others as you go – even when it's difficult. Continual practice of this is needed.
- Lead by example. Lead by setting the example that you want others to follow. Avoid kicking others while they are down.
- Speak up when that little voice says, "Will I regret not saying something about this later?"
- Be happy with the hand you are dealt – this means not always looking for the next best thing at the expense of

those on your team.
- Assume the best in others. Avoid painting a negative picture of situations when you may not have all the facts.
- Don't overreact to emotionally charged situations. Value relationships and be a loyal confidant to the best of your ability.
- Lead by developing trusted relationships with others – avoid jumping to conclusions. Trust those who you have built a relationship with, even when they tell you things you wish were not true.
- Avoid gossip. Listen for truths even when it is difficult to hear.
- Lead with human moments in mind. Recognize and embrace different perspectives. Authenticity is endearing.
- Show up on the good days and the bad, but especially on the most important days – others are watching.
- Don't take credit for other people's work, give credit where credit is due.
- Try to be inclusive of others and avoid cliques.
- Create an intentional plan for your culture – and live it. Make it part of your everyday habits. Surround yourself with those who are aligned and make you a better person. (Strong culture is my passion! Get started with a free THRIVE Model™ at www.thrivewithmb.com)
- Lead with your own style. Be bold, be wonderful, be you.

Learning from Others' Experiences

Strong leadership is essential in order to run a good business. As I've learned from a lifetime of leading (and occasionally following), there really is no one right way to lead – and everyone has their own stories that build into their leadership style. Sharing and learning from those experiences is important – and that's the beauty of this collective.

We've pulled together a stellar group of authors to create Leadership Fusion – they have written amazing chapters and shared their expertise related to their years of experience and craft. Years of learning, trying new methods, advancing new technologies, and serving clients are all collected here. Read their words. Internalize those words. Learn from them. Decide which pieces of their guidance might make the most sense to improve your leadership style or your organization.

This book is not meant to be an all-encompassing book about how to lead – we don't have enough pages for that! However, if you are seeking some fresh perspective from leaders who have driven organizational success then this book is for you. Or maybe you are looking for new ideas to develop your current leadership team or guide your organization into the 21st-century? Leadership Fusion will get you thinking outside the box and geared to try new things within your organization.

Each chapter can be read as an independent short story, written by an expert in their field. They offer ideas to raise the bar within your existing leadership development efforts. We encourage you to find golden nuggets within these pages to expand where you already have the knowledge, to challenge the "that's how we've always done it" mindset, and to strive into different realms as you try something new.

If these critical leadership areas inspire you (but also leave you thirsting for more or in need of help to get it accomplished!), then we encourage you to reach out to our thought leaders for additional help, accountability, coaching, or consulting. Definitely connect with them on LinkedIn – just knowing them will help you level up your leadership game.

We believe this book will provide you with a myriad of innovative ideas to drive your Leadership development efforts forward in a positive and effective way. Don't be afraid to think differently – that's how progress is made. Think outside the box and try new things. Join us on a journey as we explore how a little Leadership Fusion can impact your life and business in new and exciting ways.

~ Melanie Booher, INM President

I.

Leadership Simplified

Focus on What Matters

Misty Bruns, Strategic Business Leader

If you type the word "leadership" into a search engine, you will see about 3 trillion results. If that isn't enough to scare you, then you are in the right place. While this topic may seem overwhelming as we as leaders are trying to perfect our skills, think of it as the numerous opportunities we have to be better today than we were yesterday. It is not about having a natural ability to lead, nor is it about simply wanting to be a leader. Being an effective leader is about dedication and working to make yourself better so that people want to be on your team. I have been blessed to work with many different leaders along my career path – some excellent and some I would not classify as a leader at all. However, regardless of their effectiveness, I learned something from each of them and used that knowledge to help me grow in my journey as a leader. Through my experiences, I have found that while leadership is not simple, we can simplify many aspects so that we focus on what is important to keep us focused. Here is how I define leadership:

Leadership is about evolving and adjusting to what is in front of us in order to move people and organizations forward for the better.

3 trillion results and you want me to look at leadership in one sentence? Yes, I actually do. Here is why.

Evolving

We do not start our journey as strong leaders but rather we mold our style, ideas, and ability over time through education, experience, and observation. Some leaders have always risen to leadership roles and have a natural ability to have more comfort in rising to this occasion and leading well, but that doesn't mean they do not nourish this ability. There are some people born with the qualities that make them seem like more natural leaders; such as empathy, willingness to learn, and a desire to help others. However, those same qualities exist in many professions. Think about your doctor – if they don't have these qualities, you would likely look elsewhere for care. Yet, we don't necessarily think of our doctor as a leader. Leaders can be found anywhere and if we take the time to look around, we'll see it's not just about natural talent. Leadership is about the desire to take our natural talents, nurture those talents, and create something bigger than ourselves.

I started my professional career with a Fortune 500 company and was exposed quickly to numerous types of leaders – those with the biggest personalities, I thought, were the strongest leaders. What I eventually learned is that leaders who were out getting things done, working alongside their team, and listening more than talking, were actually the best leaders. They knew the most about their team and they knew how to get things done. Let's face it, getting things done is crucial for leaders to be successful!

When doing your research, you will see numerous clichés about leadership that you have likely used at some point in your career. Here are a few of my favorites:

- There is no "I" in team
- Bring me solutions, not just problems
- If we all give 110%, we'll achieve all of our goals
- Work smarter, not harder
- Failure is not an option

On the surface, most of these are true and are used in all industries and at all levels of an organization. However, they don't really tell us how to be effective leaders. The reality is that leadership looks different based on the team and the situation. Knowing that is half the battle.

The one cliché that still sticks with me to this day is that "you'll spend 80% of your time on 20% of your employees." You smile because you are now counting those employees who demand your time! While situations cannot be ignored when warranted, what I have learned over time is that that 20% don't typically require leadership – they may require time or tasks that just need to be done, but leadership alone won't fix the problem. The bigger problem then becomes less time being devoted to those employees that will benefit from your leadership, time, and development. Over time, I have evolved to focus on those that aren't always standing in line demanding my time. It may take more work to be proactive but focusing on the needs of those employees who "get it" or seem to be self-sufficient can actually be the most rewarding.

As a leader, hearing the words, "I've found another opportunity that I think is a better fit and am giving you my notice" will stop you in your tracks; especially if you hear this from a good employee. Unfortunately, once the employee is to this point, there likely isn't anything you can do to retain them. Instead, be proactive and provide as many opportunities as possible for those you want on your team and trust them by helping them to grow in their current role and beyond. When one of those employees in your 20% tells you they are leaving, accept it, wish them well, and use the opportunity to learn from that person and experience become better.

Your team knows when your main focus is on the squeaky wheel and their engagement will dwindle until they no longer respect you as a leader. Leaders aren't always liked, but leaders are respected when they hold people accountable for their actions, how they handle situations, and how they support their team.

Adjusting

Being a leader can sometimes feel like riding a roller coaster. You wait in line to get your big chance at the opportunity yet you have no idea what is in store for you! There's excitement, anxiety, fear, and even a little fun to be discovered and had. The ride takes you up and down, forwards and backward, goes at various speeds, and sometimes throws you into a dark tunnel where you have absolutely no clue what lies ahead! Embrace those times and adjust your leadership to fit each situation.

There will be situations whereas a leader, you will need to pull your team along and there will be times when you may be the one being pulled. Know the difference and adjust along the way. More importantly, appreciate those employees who pull you along the way; for they are future leaders. Naturally, we may feel a bit threatened when an individual whose title is below ours on the organizational chart is starting to shine. In the past, I often worried if they would take my place and then I wondered, "Where will that leave me?" Leadership can sometimes feel lonely, and one may feel as if they are the sole leader moving everyone forward. The reality is just the opposite. While those in leadership may feel lonely, it is not because you are alone. Likely, it is because you have put up a fence and have allowed for limited entrance.

I have held management roles where I was seen as the person to fix everything or decide upon solutions for various issues. While that sometimes felt productive, it was not enjoyable as a leader because that is not true leadership. Don't misinterpret this statement by thinking that leaders won't have to make tough decisions or that they don't have to get things done, and done on their own, each day. The reality is leadership can be messy and hard while also rewarding. Successful leaders surround themselves with the right people in the right roles.

I had an employee on my team that was smart, witty, and always looking for a new shiny object. He was always suggesting new ideas, new programs, and new ways to achieve our goals. "Great," you may be thinking, "a real go-getter!" However, when you have this person on your team and they rarely follow through with a project or idea, it becomes frustrating. I put him on a performance improvement plan to manage him out of the organization because I could not see how he fit in the organization. In reality, I had so many complaints about him that I was starting to see people question me and my ability to lead my team and I was not going to allow that. During the performance conversation, the employee was shocked at the feedback I was providing and did not understand how he was not meeting our expectations. As a leader, you don't want to be in that position because that means you have not done your job in either embracing their skill set or in properly giving them the feedback and direction they needed. I thought about our conversation and challenged my reaction. This employee provided me with several positive contributions they had made, and they were right. This employee was pivotal in my professional development because they made me adjust my way of doing things and realize that a good team is diverse and embraces unique strengths. I was trying to manage him in the same way as I managed everyone else; and, honestly, that was my fault. Once I adjusted my style and embraced this employee, we both saw what was possible and went on to lead some successful projects.

Be selective about who rides the roller coaster with you because I guarantee the ride will be more exciting and more fun! However, challenge what has "always been" and build a team that is diverse in their skills and builds on the talents of each other to create a powerful team. As you are building your team, it is important to be honest about your own shortfalls and bring that talent to your organization. Don't be threatened by the fact that others will outshine you. Instead, embrace knowing that the better we are as a whole, the better our organization is overall.

You will be more respected when your team gets things done and offers a positive contribution. When I look at my LinkedIn connections and see the growth and success of those I have worked with in the past, I am not threatened but elated when I see them shine in new roles and smile to think that as a leader, I may have had a small, little part in helping them grow, succeed, and achieve.

Front of us

Leaders keep moving forward. While we learn from the past, we don't live there. We think about what can be possible and what it takes to get there. Growth is about change and moving forward and leaders have a mindset that moves everyone forward even in difficult situations. As a leader, there will always be something to do, but I challenge you to be intentional about what those things are so that they are supporting the organization's mission and vision. If you do not know what those two things are for your organization, find them and build your plan to support them.

I often advise clients to write down their big goals and review them often – some think it can be tedious and others believe it has guided them to be better leaders. Have you ever looked at the clock only to realize the day is all but over, yet you still have a full to-do list requiring your attention? Those days are a reality and will happen, but if we allow them to become the norm in our schedule, we will not be able to grow and will not be proactive in moving us forward. I love making lists and crossing off items to feel that sense of accomplishment! However, one day I realized that my list was all about tasks rather than goals and development. I was not fully challenging myself to do and be better as a leader...I started creating a list that supported the big ideas and goals and quickly found that I began to grow as a leader and was able to share that with my team. I created long-term goals, but goals that I could accomplish within five years. I was amazed at how my focus and priorities changed!

You might be thinking, "That sounds great, but how can you add that into your already packed day?" You evaluate all of those tasks to determine what is necessary and what is nice to have. Create metaphorical buckets in your mind for what you are required to get done, what you can delegate to your team, and what is simply not necessary. Initially, this will add time to your day, and maybe your evenings, while you figure out the highest priorities. Reports, charts, and status updates are a great place to start because these tasks are likely already being done because they always have been. I spent hours a month on an HR report that went to various leaders reporting our results from the prior month. Rarely did I receive any feedback on the report and it was never a topic of discussion in the monthly staff meeting. So, I stopped doing it. Guess what? No one asked about it and the business continued to run. This is the type of task that I challenge you to evaluate and determine if it is actually needed or if there is a more streamlined approach. I took that time and intentionally used it for my development and my time to focus on my team's development to move us forward to be better partners.

In order to focus on what is in front of us, you will have to be proactive in thinking about "what if?" Not allowing ourselves the opportunity and time to think about what we can offer as leaders is a true disservice to your team and to your organization. As a leader, I love doing this! Offering suggestions for ways to run the organization more efficiently or seeking better ways to develop the team is what gets me the most excited as a leader. Do you ever wake up in the middle of the night and have this great idea but by morning, you either have forgotten it or it doesn't seem as brilliant as it did at 3 am? We've all heard it before but many don't do it – keep a notebook by your bed and with you throughout the day to jot down ideas. Some ideas may come to be, while others may never leave the paper. And that's okay! That is how we keep those ideas in front of us and keep us moving forward.

People and Situations

Be the bigger person in EVERY situation. Yes, we are all human and there will be people that will test you more than you ever thought possible. Even with that person, dig deep down into your core and be the bigger person. Here is the thing to remember – when you are making decisions for the betterment of the organization, you are not going to make everyone happy and you will upset people. Your goal as a leader should never be to make everyone happy. Why? Because it is a goal that simply cannot be achieved. It is impossible to please everyone. Accept that and know how to handle the situations of disappointment so that you can remain calm and respectful.

Let me explain why this is critical. Have you ever appeared as a witness in court or sat through a six-hour deposition? I don't wish that "fun" on anyone, but know that as a leader, your comments and actions should be made as if you had to repeat them in court. You may be in a conversation that is quickly turning south with an employee saying everything wrong and your gut is to respond in kind. Unfortunately, it does not matter what the employee said before your reply to them because your comment is all that will be remembered or shared. This is a tough reality to face, and know that it will challenge you at some point in your career if it has not already!

My challenging employee came fairly early in my career while managing multiple labor contracts. I was naïve in thinking that every situation could be "fixed" with a conversation and a handshake. I learned quickly that not everyone will be honest and upfront and found myself sitting before lawyers having to explain to them, on record, why I called this employee an idiot. Regardless of what I thought of this person and how they handled the situation, I should have been the bigger person. There's no coming back to defending your decision as a leader when the only thing everyone around you knows is that you stooped to the level of name-calling. No matter what transpired before, you are now the one being questioned on your leadership ability. So, don't fall into the fight, don't puff your ego, and don't demand to have the last word. Be a leader, be respectful, and manage the situation as if you would have to repeat yourself on record.

You likely did not hear about all of the tough things you may experience as a leader because those are the things people don't particularly like to think about. Your first difficult coaching conversation, your first termination meeting, or the first time you have an employee break down in tears in your office are all things that you really can't plan or prepare for ahead of time. As leaders, we get excited about the challenges of being more efficient and the challenge of helping our team exceed goals. Remember that the same tenacity, the same heart, and the same dedication will be needed in all of these situations. Stay on the track to do what is right, be authentic, and always treat others with respect.

Better

You won't see perfection in anything, and when leaders can take that pressure away and focus on being better each day, they are more successful. I'm not implying that you won't experience setbacks in your career because I am here to tell you that you will. Learn from those experiences and take that knowledge with you to do better each day. Organizations are constantly changing to meet the demands of their customers, demands of growth, and demands of changing employees. Let's face it, we can all look back at those first few jobs we held, how we managed those first few teams, and how we handled those first few challenges in our careers. If you can't honestly say you are a better leader today, then I'd challenge that you are not learning from your experiences.

Becoming better is not easy and often takes some deep, inner searching and acceptance of our own shortcomings. If we cannot see that we all have room for improvement, then there is no hope of becoming stronger leaders. I could fill a book just with the stories I have experienced from employees and often I reflect upon them to help me grow. The reality is that some employees are just not the right fit for your team, but they have provided you with an experience that has brought you to where you are today.

Unfortunately, not everyone has the desire to make the team or organization better. While those individuals may teach us something, it is not necessary to continue their employment. The reality is that some people have no interest in seeing the team move forward. I've had coffee thrown at me, been called more names than I can remember, been threatened, and broken up numerous altercations. Those are the situations where you learn and move on quickly; otherwise, you are back to managing versus leading. I have worked with law enforcement, government agencies, and ex-spouses all in the hopes of helping employees to no avail. As leaders, you have likely experienced similar circumstances that you would like to forget. However, with all the negative come to the experiences that I would not trade for the world! When an employee lets you be a part of their family, calls you when they get their first promotion, or simply wants to meet over a drink to catch up, embrace and revel in those moments and those individuals; for they are the people you should thank for helping to shape you as a leader.

Leadership is a coveted position of privilege. No one but the leader can facilitate the change and growth of each person in a company towards one common goal. As a leader, I am passionate about self-development and helping others to see their own potential. I also believe there is a difference between training and development. Training is typically task-oriented, involving things such as using an IT system or learning steps to perform a specific job function. Development is about exploring, using that knowledge to challenge, and ultimately, learning and doing better. There is not one piece of advice, one assessment, or one mentor that will provide you with the golden arrow to becoming the perfect leader. Instead, take a little bit from each person you meet and interact with, each situation you experience, and each assessment that you do to learn and grow to move you towards being better tomorrow than you are today.

Misty Bruns

For the last twenty years, Misty Bruns has been a leader who helps people achieve success!

As a businesswoman with a diverse and impressive background in various levels of professionalism, she has experience working with Coca-Cola Enterprises, Payless ShoeSource, and Pak-Rite Industries, to name a few. Her experience ranges in leadership roles amongst larger Fortune 500 companies to family owned organizations in both union and nonunion environments.

Her impressive career started with a B.S from Miami University in Human Resource Management and Organizational behavior. While at Miami, she volunteered as a victim advocate and spoke to local school age students about ways they can use their leadership skills to help others. Life-long learning is a core passion that her mother, Donna, instilled from a young age. Misty believes this helped her achieve the success she has in her career. She holds a Masters degree in Education in Human Resource Development from Xavier University and recently earned her MBA from the University of Dayton. Misty has an SPHR certification from The Society for Human Resource Management (SHRM) that she has kept current throughout her career.

Though her skills are clearly diverse, she specializes in planning for businesses to include leadership development, succession planning, employee relations, financial evaluation, as well as start up operations. As a professional, her passions lie in building the right teams, offering opportunities for development and growth, and coaching high-level executives on the most effective means to execute their goals.

Working in numerous industries such as retail, wholesale, logistics, and automotive gives Misty a unique business knowledge that she likes to use when giving back to her community through various volunteer opportunities. Misty has also served on many boards over the years, mentored numerous students, and coordinates events to benefit local charities.

Apart from her expansive professional accomplishments, Misty resides outside of Dayton, OH with her husband, Joseph, and her two children, Eli & Riley, around whom her world revolves! Cheering on her kids at their various events is her greatest joy. They love to spend their time at the beach as a way to keep their family "anchored."

CONNECT WITH MISTY BRUNS:

https://www.linkedin.com/in/mistybruns937/

2.

Inclusive Leadership

Joi Turner, DEI Business Partner | Strategist

What do you think it means to be an inclusive leader? Take a moment to use this space to write down five behaviors that you believe represent inclusive leadership.

_____

_____

_____

_____

_____

Before digging into what you wrote, it's important to note that there is no one-size-fits-all blueprint when it comes to being an inclusive leader. These behaviors are also not specific to someone in a "management" role. Anyone can be a leader. So, let's take a look – what does inclusive leadership actually mean? Inclusive leadership is acknowledging your viewpoint and utilizing the diversity around you to collaborate and encourage differing thoughts and perspectives.

As leaders, it's easy to fall into old habits and behaviors when it comes to strategy, development, and execution. However, organizations across the world are beginning to recognize the value of amplifying voices that may not always be as easily heard. There is a staggering amount of innovation happening right now that can be directly linked to diversity and inclusion. When I say diversity, in this case, I want to focus more on the diversity of thought. Everywhere you look, you'll find that people are being presented with new opportunities daily. We're seeing fewer degree restrictions, generational shifts in management, and an overall cultural shift when it comes to what a traditional workplace looks like. These types of changes aren't easy, but they are worth it.

A great way to start this conversation is by asking yourself, why does this matter? Why is it important to you? Honestly, it can be difficult to express an answer to these questions when beginning the study of inclusive leadership. I had a hard time accepting my "why." It took a while for me to really articulate why this particular work matters to me. This is a safe space so I'll share it with you all here and now. As I was moving through my first few roles in Corporate America, I never really felt seen. As a woman, and especially as a black woman, I didn't have a space where I genuinely felt I could contribute to the conversation or share ideas that may help with overall team success. Were people nice? Sure. However, did I have that leader that empowered me and gave me the support I needed to feel seen, valued, and heard? Rarely. This is a sad reality, and quite frankly, unacceptable. Every goal that I've set for myself as I've moved along my career journey is one that positions me to do better than what I've experienced. I never want to be the leader that someone feels uncomfortable around. I never want to be the leader that someone feels they have to hide a part of themselves from. Perhaps in some ways, this goal is selfish, but I do believe it's mutually beneficial. I can be the leader I always needed while building up a team of other leaders who can truly impact change. I focus on being an inclusive leader so that it replaces the current status quo. We can always do better. We can always be better. I want to show my team what inclusive leadership looks like on a daily basis so that as they lead, they're aware of the behaviors and can make them their own.

Think about your experiences; I challenge you to really put some thought into your why. This can, and likely will, take some time; but think about why this transformation matters. Think about things that you've seen in the past that haven't been modeled to you with an inclusive mindset, and what you would do now to change that. I've found that when you're able to relate these behaviors to personal experiences, it's easier to adapt to them. I don't want to overwhelm you with too many takeaways at once, so I am going to keep this as basic (yet impactful) as possible. The goal here is to lay the foundation for what's next, not solve every problem at once.

Now, let's take a look at what you wrote above for the five behaviors that you believe represent inclusive leadership. Do any of your answers reflect incorporating fresh, new perspectives into your day-to-day decision-making? Are you getting feedback from the team about how the team should operate? It may seem like a simple concept, but oftentimes we forget that the best feedback that we can receive as leaders to help improve processes and drive engagement, retention, and success, comes directly from the teams we hope to improve. This may look different for every leader. Some leaders may opt to hold focus groups to gauge how their team is feeling, while others may send out surveys so that there is a level of anonymity. Others still may hold 1:1 sessions – all of which are effective ways of gathering feedback, which is the key. Can we effectively lead a team if we aren't giving them an opportunity to share their experiences and offer feedback? Opening up this channel of communication not only acts as a morale booster, as people begin to feel more valued and heard, but it also produces results. You'll begin to see an increase in productivity, engagement, key performance indicators, revenue, and overall employee satisfaction. There are limitless possibilities for innovation that live within our teams, but we have to be willing to step aside and let them contribute to the conversation.

Your list should be looking good by now! Let's talk more about the conversations we mentioned before. It's critical that when we, as leaders, invite new talent into these conversations, leaders are doing so with open ears as well as open minds. No matter what industry you're in, the size of your team, or your role within your organization – there is always room for growth and improvement. Perhaps you've been in this role for twenty years and you can't quite figure out how to take your team to the next level. Or maybe you're new to the role and want to make sure that your team is as successful as possible. While both of these scenarios are different, there is a shared solution. **Talk to your teams.** Talk about their current experiences, past experiences, ways to iterate on current processes, and ways to improve. Ask them about your managerial style and ways that you can improve upon the way(s) in which you manage. The scope of your daily responsibilities may look different than the teams that you support, so why not build processes based on the opinions of those doing the footwork? Additionally, as you're getting to know your teams and building these best practices that support inclusion, you may begin to recognize why certain processes didn't work out before. One of the things many leaders overlook is understanding how their team members learn and process information. There are so many learning style assessments that you can have your teams take to ensure you're presenting information in a way that resonates with them all, inclusivity extends to the ways in which we present information. Personally, my go-to is on educationplanner.org, where you can find the "What's Your Learning Style" quiz under "Self-Assessments."

If this framework of openness and candid conversations isn't one that your team is used to, there is another important behavior to highlight that, ideally, needs to come first – building trust. Inclusive leadership relies heavily on the thoughts and opinions of others, but in order to have those conversations, individuals have to feel comfortable and safe. This doesn't apply or refer to just physical safety; although that is also equally important. Instead, it is a matter of psychological safety. According to the Center for Creative Leadership, psychological safety is the belief that you won't be punished or humiliated for speaking up with ideas, questions, concerns, or mistakes. Many times, people feel as though they have to hide some or most of who they truly are in the workplace. This leads to burnout and attrition. As leaders, specifically inclusive leaders, we have to encourage authenticity and get to know the people working around us. You'll notice that as we build on these inclusive leadership behaviors, it almost always comes back to the conversation and it's important to acknowledge that they may not all be what you want to hear. In order to build trust, we have to get comfortable with being uncomfortable. Ask your team about how you could better support them. Find out if there are practices or elements of leadership that they would like to see from you that aren't a part of your current routine. Make a solid plan to implement those suggestions. Talk to the person with a different religious background, and ask team members about family dynamics and weekend plans. In short: build relationships. The more you work to intentionally build meaningful relationships in the workplace, the more open and honest your team will be with you. Another great way to build trust is to admit when you've made a mistake. Did you try to build a process that was ineffective? Did you fall into a trap of unconscious bias? Did you forget to cascade an important memo to your team? Whatever the case may be, make sure that you're candid with your team. Lead by example. If we can admit that we, as leaders, also make mistakes, the feeling of psychological safety will increase amongst the team.

If your list has other behaviors so far, no worries! Remember, this isn't one-size-fits-all. While the structure of your teams may be different and the organizations may vary, an inclusive leader demonstrates a level of uniformity when it comes to advocacy for the people around us. Advocacy is one of the inclusive leadership behaviors that really stands out. Remember how we talked about having to get comfortable being uncomfortable? That hasn't changed. If you notice someone's voice being silenced, value not being placed on someone's opinion, or someone being excluded – say something. We can't consider ourselves inclusive leaders if we aren't showing up for everyone. Is it hard work? Yes. Is it worth it? Absolutely. It takes a lot of courage to challenge what has been the norm for so long. It also takes courage to admit when someone else may be better suited for a role, project, or to answer a particular question. Bring that person in, and be the leader that helps that team member find their voice. As you begin to advocate for others, you'll notice that you're also developing the next generation of leaders. That person that you stood up for will notice and they'll be able to apply that well-modeled behavior if they're ever in a similar situation.

Let's pause for a moment. What are your takeaways so far? What are some of the behaviors you feel need to exist in order to be an inclusive leader?

It's easy to talk about behaviors when everything is in black and white, but what does the application look like in practice? How do you take these words and turn them into a plan of action? So much of this work is about behaviors and mindset shifts, and the most practical way to adjust these current behaviors and build new habits is to set goals and create action plans. A popular acronym used in Corporate America right now is SMART Goals. A SMART Goal is a goal that you're putting in place that is Specific, Measurable, Attainable, Relevant, and Timely. If you want to meet with each member of your team over the next two weeks to get to know them more, create a goal for it. Build out as many goals as you need but make sure they're SMART. If you need help kick-starting some goals of your own, ask yourself these questions:

S	• Specific • What EXACTLY do you want to acheive?
M	• Measurable • How will you know when you've acheived it?
A	• Attainable • Is this something you have control over?
R	• Relevant • Why is this applicaple?
T	• Timely • When do you want to acheive your goal?

Some additional questions you can ask yourself are:

- *What do you want to accomplish and what steps will you take to get there?*
- *Who do you hope to impact?*
- *What changes do you want to see within your team and organization?*
- *And of course, never lose sight of your "why"*

This is not an exhaustive list of questions, but hopefully, it helps you begin to look at where your team or organization is now, and create a plan that helps drive you forward.

After talking about a number of behaviors you can use to become a more inclusive leader, let's revise your original list. This chapter provides another safe space to write out what you think it means to be an inclusive leader. Do you want to change anything? Do you want to keep everything as is? Whatever the case may be, do it! As leaders, it's important to iterate over and over until you find what works for you and the teams you support. This exercise of identifying inclusive behaviors is no different. Take some time to think about these behaviors if you need to. When you're ready, start practicing these daily and take note of the shift you see in your organizational culture. This shift won't happen overnight and it takes practice and consistency. Be patient with yourself, and employ grace. Inclusive leadership is just one piece of the overall diversity, equity, and inclusion framework, but as you continue on this path to inclusivity, you will notice a transformation within yourself and your team. It takes time, but it ***will*** come.

Joi Turner

Joi Turner (she/her) is a Diversity, Equity, and Inclusion Business Partner. Certified in DEI in the Workplace and Inclusive and Ethical Leadership from the University of South Florida, Joi is focused on DEI strategy and execution. A leader in her organization, she continues to develop initiatives to make an inclusive and equitable workplace a reality for everyone. With a background in Learning and Development, Joi has a decade of experience facilitating several types of new-hire and developmental training. She has also managed teams of trainers across multiple industries including finance, retail, and healthcare.

A Cincinnati native, Joi gives back to the community as a YP Board member for Big Brothers, Big Sisters, and the YP Professional Leadership Chair for Urban League of Greater Southwestern Ohio. Joi enjoys spending time with her family, especially her son Jackson, listening to 90's R&B, and traveling. During the pandemic, Joi also realized she had a passion for DIY home remodeling projects and interior decorating.

CONNECT WITH JOI TURNER:

https://www.linkedin.com/in/s-joi-turner/

3.

Leading with Intention

Mike Sipple Jr, Co-Founder and CEO, Talent Magnet Institute®, CEO, Centennial

People are unhappy. Specifically, they are stressed, worried, sad, and angry. You probably don't need statistics to back this up – a quick look around and an observant eye will verify this quickly – but Gallup has done the work of quantifying this unhappiness for us.

Gallup's State of the Global Workplace 2021 report has informed us that across the globe 41% of people experience daily worry, 43% deal with daily stress, 24% admit to daily anger, and 25% struggle with daily sadness.[1]

This is discouraging. Being worried, stressed, angry and sad is not a good formula for a meaningful life. What's more, it's not a good formula for being the best person you can be. These statistics represent real people who live near you, possibly live with you, and they may even be you.

How do you respond to these statistics as a leader? How can we expect dedicated, quality work from people who are emotionally wrung out? Clearly, these statistics need to change. We can't continue to drive work through people who feel disconnected, lack motivation, and are generally unhappy.

If you are reading this book, you are a leader with a desire to lead and to lead well. You want results that you can be proud of and that make a difference. You are looking for solutions and the answers to the questions, "How can I lead in a way that is meaningful and motivating?" "How can I diminish unhappiness and increase satisfaction?" It starts with you. It starts with getting personal. It starts with seeing your employees as individuals with very real goals, challenges, and dreams.

"Leading with Intention means taking action. I have a gift for you, the people who read this book because you know that leadership matters.

Visit: https://www.talentmagnet.com/fusion" ~Mike Sipple, Jr.

For decades, the world has led through policies, data, and technology. Utilizing a one-size-fits-all mentality of leadership is not working. Each person is unique, and the leaders of today need to manage with that reality in mind. People who are in a position to impact others must start managing as mentors. No one should think of themselves as superior, but rather as a guide or a coach.

Labeling a manager and boss as negative is unjust and unfair. In fact, becoming a manager and a boss is on many people's lists of goals. The current negativity associated with the words "boss" and "manager" is all done to create cliques and interest. Rebuff this trend by being an awe-inspiring and encouraging boss, rather than a bossy and uncaring one. Bad bosses do what they want to do without considering the other people involved.

Conversely, true mentors and awe-inspiring bosses are very interested in other people – other people as individuals.

A mentor's entire focus is to better the people who come to them for help and guidance. They coach and encourage people to become better versions of themselves. It is essential to have managers who know enough about their people that they can challenge, support, and encourage them in the best ways possible.

What is your mentor or coach persona?

Think carefully of someone in your life who fulfilled the role of meaningful mentor/or coach. For me, that person springs to mind easily. My 11th and 12th-grade History teacher lived out this mentor leadership admirably. Ms. Gregory cared about each student as an individual. That level of individual care had a huge impact on my life.

I can clearly remember being frustrated by her because I felt an unfair level of accountability. She would ask me questions, challenge me, and not accept excuses that seemed to work just fine with other teachers. Do you have a Ms. Gregory in your life? Maybe a relative, a coach, or a teacher like me?

More than twenty years later, I can see Ms. Gregory's leadership style. I can see how she made it personal so that I became a better person. She got involved in my journey and took me on new and better paths. She pushed me to go beyond my natural comfort zones because she saw the potential that lived inside of me.

– LEADERSHIP IN ACTION –

Ms. Gregory's innate leadership style is one to learn from. Consider which statements can be said of you.

- She called out specific areas she knew I could improve on.
- She made me work hard.
- She coached me in my areas of weakness.
- She leveraged my strengths.
- She made me redo work that wasn't my best.
- She challenged me to do things I didn't want to do.
- She cared.
- She was proud of me.
- She saw results.
- She made me a better human. (Although it took a while!)

Ms. Gregory challenged, supported, and encouraged me as someone who really cared. Decades later, I still think of her as an outstanding example of the kind of leader I want to be. She made leadership personal. She took time to invest in me, learned my strengths and weaknesses, and then helped me unlock the potential that she knew was already inside of me.

I was not "Student #345", I was Mike Sipple Jr., an energetic teenager, lover of baseball and basketball, eager to raise my hand – either to participate or in an attempt to make the entire classroom laugh – a friend to all, and technology-enthusiast. She knew I'd rather goof off than apply myself to a writing assignment, but her belief in me made me want to work harder than I did for any other teacher. She helped shape that goofy high schooler into the leader that I am today.

Individual Leadership in the Workplace

Let's translate this individual leadership to leading in the workplace. Learn how to challenge, support, and encourage your peers, colleagues, direct reports, and other work relationships so that everyone is more connected and satisfied.

The rest of the chapter will look at how you can transform the leadership that overflows to everyone around you to make it personal and effective. You can be as impactful as that special teacher/coach/mentor/grandparent was for you. You can help others be their greatest self. Along the way, there will be practical suggestions to help you start your transformation today.

As mentioned at the beginning of the chapter, there are a lot of negative emotions that people are dealing with every day. Another sobering statistic is that 80% of the global workforce feels disengaged[2]. That's completely unacceptable. Many arguments can be made for the reasons behind this, but that doesn't really solve any problems.

Employees who are unengaged will leave; seeking connection and satisfaction in another organization. Reports such as Gallup's State of the Global Workplace are very eye-opening. However, because the data doesn't reach our desk for months after it's collected, the people who responded that they were unhappy and disengaged felt that way six months ago. How much damage has been done during the time that passed while the report was synthesized, organized, formatted, and communicated? Now is the time to be proactive. Today is the day to start. Start with a conversation – several, in fact. Have conversations with individuals to truly and fully understand them as individuals, and then support them with their individual journeys.

Schedule time for conversations. Create real conversations with real discussions. Getting to know people as individuals requires two-way communication. You need fully engaged conversations where you ask open-ended questions and then listen – truly listen. In the past, you may have done a lot of talking and had a lot of meetings, but you need to go further to find out more about people as individuals. You must be authentic and vulnerable as well. Leaders, awe-inspiring bosses, lead by example and are unafraid to be open, honest, transparent, and vulnerable.

Conversations Require Active Listening

Let's start by addressing active listening. Don't skim over this. Active listening is half the formula – I could even argue it's more than half the formula – when you plan to lead with compassion and impact. The first step in active listening is turning off as many distractions as possible.

I get distracted easily. So, for me, I have quite a checklist for eliminating possible distractions. I really shouldn't face an open door or a window. There is just too much life happening on the other side of windows and doors that I tend to find awfully intriguing. For instance, right now there is a preschool class taking a walk on the sidewalk outside my office and I find it so captivating. The little boy with the red hair reminds me of my oldest son and the one little girl is skipping along and appears totally confident and at peace with the world. It's so sweet, so fun, and so distracting! This is not the making of an intentional conversation – or a finished chapter on leadership.

Besides the life going on outside of my office, there are plenty of distractions within arm's reach – my phone, watch, and computer are an endless source of notifications. The intent of your conversation is to invest in people as individuals. To do this, you must treat each person as valued, heard, and understood. That is appropriately conveyed, in large part, by giving them 100% of your attention when you are talking. Turn off notifications or go a step further and leave your devices outside the room you are meeting in.

Another practical tip for staying focused and showing your interest is to ask follow-up questions and repeat back what you hear. This confirms for the other person that you are truly paying attention and you care enough to be sure you understand what they are saying. This also helps to solidify in your own mind what you are hearing. Repetition is a great memory tool.

Conversations for Impact

At this point, you should feel prepared and eager to have intentional conversations. My experience has shown me time and time again that there are several topics that must be crystal clear if your employees are going to feel valued, heard, and understood as an individual. The two topics that stand out as most critical are unpacked below. These conversation topics will go a long way in showing your care for each employee as an individual and result in more engaged, happier people.

1. How does the individual's role align with the mission of the organization?
2. Knowing the personal and professional goals of each individual.

The Individual's Role and the Mission of the Organization

If a person doesn't realize how their role aligns with the mission of the organization there will be a great lack of motivation. People need to know what value they bring to the company to feel that they have a purpose.

Clearly communicating the absolute impact of someone's role and how their role lines up with the organization's objectives will move someone from a black hole of uncertainty to an empowered player who has significant importance.

It is a great privilege of yours, as a leader, to highlight what a tremendous asset they are. You might be wondering how leaders might communicate this to their staff. It is vital to have an open line of communication by keeping channels of communication open and honest. The individual should leave the conversation knowing they are not a drain on the company, but rather a very important part of helping the business, and their peers, succeed. This mind shift can make a huge difference to their work satisfaction. No one wants to feel unwanted or unnecessary. Show them their significance!

Personal and Professional Goals

The next conversation you should have is about personal and professional goals. Knowing where your employees dream of going – literally and figuratively – makes a tremendous difference when you are helping them achieve their goals to their greatest satisfaction. Discovering what is important to them is the way to get to know them as individuals.

Not all employees will want to go into great detail about their personal life, but allow them to share with you what they are comfortable with. Once you know their goals, do what you can to help them reach those goals. That may come in the form of additional training at work, connecting them with someone who can advance that dream, or simply being a voice of support. Help them see how their dream can be achieved through their work. This personal investment makes the difference in someone feeling like a cog in a machine, rather than an individual with great potential.

The unfortunate reality is that someone's long-term dreams may require a move outside of your company. They may have a professional dream that isn't available within your organization. Or, they may have personal dreams of moving closer to family or shifting to a part-time role. Both of these may require a move. How will you feel about this? How can you spend time investing in an employee only to have them move away?

Retention is always a priority, but there is another, equally important priority. Your goal should be to create ambassadors for your organization. How does an organization, and its leaders, foster this kind of supportive culture; even when it means that your employees might leave?

Your role as a mentor, coach, and manager is really to help unlock the human potential that lives inside of your people. Your investment in people is for their growth and advancement. It is possible that you could so thoroughly support an employee that they move on to another organization. However, they'll move on, knowing that the leadership and the experience they had at your company were so amazing that it's worth telling others about.

Don't be an employee's ceiling of opportunity. Instead, identify and remove barriers and any potential ceilings that may exist. You can help them see in themselves their fullest potential.

The best exiting employee is one who has nothing but incredible things to say about your company and its leadership. Having an ambassador who happily refers prospective clients and future workers to you is a win of a different kind. Sure, you'd like your employee to stay with your organization and do great work for you, but if their dreams pull them away, don't you want them to leave knowing you are part of the reason they are able to fulfill their dreams? This kind of supportive and encouraging culture is not lost on people and won't be forgotten quickly.

– LEADERSHIP IN ACTION –

Be the leader who is remembered for supporting, encouraging, and caring for them more than anyone else they worked for, or with, in the past.

When you sit down one-on-one with your employees to learn about their personal and professional goals, here are some questions that should be asked:

- What part of your job do you really enjoy?
- What training do you think would be beneficial for the next twelve months?
- Which work responsibilities do you find most challenging?
- What is one area in the company you would like to see improvement? Do you have any ideas on how that could be improved?
- What are three to five professional goals you would like to set for yourself this year?
- What else would be helpful for me and this team to know in order to support you and help you be your best?
- What do you do to feel refreshed?
- What motivates you?

Regular Conversations for Lasting Impact

These conversations should be a regular part of your meetings with your employees. Care for them, nurture them, and invest in them. Making this a regular rhythm will establish your standing and relationship as a person who is safe to talk to as well as an ally to help you achieve greater satisfaction.

As you start these conversations, you may need to emphasize your desire to hear honest, thoughtful answers. A three-word answer is not what you're after. Make it clear that you'd really like to hear their honest opinions, their true dreams, and their biggest frustrations. Of course, this is assuming that you are asking because you care and not to use it against them in any way. Your intentions need to be virtuous and communicated appropriately to individuals.

Getting to know your people is what good leadership is all about. That's the only way to create a culture that motivates people long-term and empowers them to perform at their best. It is critical that you reciprocate the openness that you have worked hard to create and foster. In fact, take the lead with a real example and be fully authentic so they can see who you are and what motivates and drives you. Lead from the front, and by example. This will help your employees follow suit easily.

Gratitude – So Simple and Yet So Powerful

Beyond conversations, another powerful way to boost engagement is through gratitude. This underutilized "tool" should be a natural extension of your care and compassion for the people you work with. Whether it's your peer, a colleague, a business partner or your own supervisor, a simple and small word of gratitude can brighten anyone's day.

More importantly, there are good ways to express your appreciation, and then there are better ways. The way I used to express gratitude fell into the "good" category before I learned that my gratitude had a greater impact when a little more thought was put into it. Any gratitude is welcome but let's go the extra step and be specific.

Make your words of appreciation specific if you want them to stick and resonate. For years, I would regularly say things like "Thanks for all you do" or "You are a Rock Star" (this is my favorite). I also used phrases like, "You are such an awesome team member," or "I am so thankful for people like you in my life." It was all heartfelt and genuine, but it lacked impact. Those phrases didn't pack a punch if you will. Where was the problem? My phrases were too generic.

My appreciative words could apply to the lady who cuts my hair, the teenager who mows my grass, or my wife who leads, serves, and runs, well – just about anything. In the workplace, those same words were directed to the person on my team who just created a "Raving Fan-worthy" client experience, to the individual on my team who took a risk, or to the team member who helped another employee accomplish a milestone. Those simple words "thanks for all you do" start to lose their punch when it is conveniently handed it out in all situations.

Instead, it is important to learn how to be specific. Work to make the compliment(s) personal. The recipient of gratitude should feel the value of the intention behind the words and compliments. So, instead of something generic, what might be said is as follows: "[First name], I saw how hard you worked to present our progress and deliverables to the client. You presented with such strong confidence. I appreciate you and your hard work so much. Thank you!" Yes, it might take some extra thought, but in less than a minute, appreciation is more fully expressed to someone who is clearly and truly deserving. Or, gratitude could look like this: "[First name], thank you for recommending we take a different approach last week in the all-team meeting. Hearing you share what you did gives me great

| 59

confidence that our team members feel safe to share what is on their minds when they feel it creates a better outcome."

– LEADERSHIP IN ACTION –

Here are two challenges for you to help you exercise your gratitude muscle. This week, send two thank you notes and give two public statements of gratitude. Now when I say public, this can be a "thank you" to another family member with the family present or it could be a post on social media where you know the recipient will see it. It could also be in a meeting at work where you take sixty seconds to acknowledge the hard work of someone in the room. Remember, please be specific.

In your two thank you notes, let each person know how they have made your life better. Specifically, write what they did – big or small – that had a meaningful impact on you. This may be long overdue, but gratitude truly has no expiration date.

For your public statement of gratitude, keep it brief but meaningful. This is not the time to make up for the past five years when there were no words of appreciation. This is just the starting point. Make it specific and make it authentic.

Don't know where to start? Here are a few ideas to help:

- Thank you for giving your time and talents to make _____ happen.
- Thank you for being a great example for others to learn and follow.
- Thank you for the work you did on _____.
- Thank you for overcoming objections in this way.
- Thank you for adding _____ to our team.

The Power of Real-time Feedback and Leading

Lastly, let's hit on real-time feedback. This is a game-changer if you want people to perform to the best of their ability. Providing real-time feedback will allow people to make small changes to their work that will inevitably lead to huge improvements over time. If you wait for months to share feedback – maybe waiting for a scheduled review – there's a good chance that you will have multiple things that you want to address and it can overwhelm the person receiving the feedback. Not to mention that you've just lost the past few months of time that could have been months of working towards improvement.

Remember that you aren't providing feedback to be critical or to make someone feel inferior to you. Your feedback should be motivated by a desire to see people become a better version of themselves. You are providing feedback because you care.

Let's Get Real

Someone may recently start struggling to hit deadlines and through a conversation, built on regular and intentional conversations, you might learn that the employee's child was just diagnosed with diabetes. If they are trying to juggle the emotional stress of this diagnosis while managing work as normal, this is understandably going to affect that employee's work performance. Lead with empathy and figure out how you can support them through this hard time.

Someone else may be struggling to deliver quality work in a

particular area. Rather than assuming they are incompetent, brainstorm ideas with them in order to improve their skills and provide different tools. Have them swap responsibilities with another coworker who has strength in an area that they do not. There may be a number of solutions that come up when feedback is freely given and received.

There could also be someone else who simply can't keep up the pace that you require at your company. Have conversations about this. Help them in any way that you can, knowing that in the end, they might not be a long-term fit. However, if they need to leave, their departure should never be a surprise. There should be multiple conversations and the employee should feel cared for throughout the process. You want to create an ambassador for that employee, right? Consider helping them find a new position or a new company. I have done this many times in my career and both the past team members and our team have benefited greatly from being so supportive.

Start Reversing the Statistics Today

Leading with your focus on individual care is a shift that needs to happen. You should desire to be a talent magnet who not only attracts and retains great people but who helps them achieve all their goals and reach their fullest potential. As researched in Gallup's State of the Global Workplace 2021 report, "80% of employees are disengaged/unengaged" should simply not be acceptable in your organization. In fact, it shouldn't even be true in society at all.[3]

The statistics of employee engagement and mental health do not have to be where and what they are today. Leading through authentic conversations, gratitude, and real-time feedback will create an environment in that people thrive. It will have a life-changing effect on those you lead, manage, and support.

Don't be afraid to tell your employees that you care about them. Don't be afraid to walk with them and support them on their personal journey. Don't be afraid to find out more about who they are. It's in those times of intentional care that true leadership happens.

Notes

1. Gallup, Inc. "State of the Global Workplace Report." Gallup.com, Gallup INC., 20 Nov. 2021, https://www.gallup.com/workplace/349484/state-of-the-global-workplace.aspx.
2. Gallup, Inc. "State of the Global Workplace Report." Gallup.com, Gallup INC., 20 Nov. 2021, https://www.gallup.com/workplace/349484/state-of-the-global-workplace.aspx.
3. Gallup, Inc. "State of the Global Workplace Report." Gallup.com, Gallup INC., 20 Nov. 2021, https://www.gallup.com/workplace/349484/state-of-the-global-workplace.aspx.

Mike Sipple Jr.

"Leading with Intention means taking action. I have a gift for you, the people who read this book, because you know that leadership matters.

https://www.talentmagnet.com/fusion" ~Mike Sipple, Jr.

Mike Sipple, Jr. is the Co-Founder and CEO of the Talent Magnet Institute® and believes deeply in TMI's mission to unlock human potential. TMI is a people-centric leadership and management training and support for your journey.

Mike is also the CEO of Centennial Executive Search & Talent Strategy, with over a half century of experience building vibrant leadership teams for companies from over 16 countries.

Mike and his dad co-founded TMI after Centennial's clients continued to seek strategic and leadership advice from Centennial beyond executive search. Including coaching next-generation leaders, supporting growth in early to mid-career professionals, and supporting high-performing teams to lead with intention and create healthy, supportive cultures.

Both businesses strive to help leaders achieve their personal and organizational mission and vision.

Mike is a sought-after speaker and moderator for associations, executive peer groups, conferences, and organizations on Becoming a Talent Magnet®, Courageous Leadership, Steps to Re-Energizing Teams, and The Great REALIZATION, and various other leadership topics.

Mike writes and speaks; these writing and speaking engagements can be viewed or listened to at:

- Thrive Global
- Business Courier Leadership Trust
- The Opposite of Small Talk
- Punk Rock HR
- Life in the Leadership Lane
- HR Social Hour
- HR Chat
- Impact Makers

and various other publications and podcasts.

> "Leadership is a journey, and you don't have to walk it alone." ~Mike Sipple, Jr.

CONNECT WITH MIKE SIPPLE JR.:

https://www.linkedin.com/in/mikesipplejr/

https://www.talentmagnet.com/

www.CentennialInc.com

4.

Your Employees are Not Your Friends

Lacy Starling, Entrepreneur, Consultant, Educator

About five years into owning my logistics business, I was eviscerated by a 360-degree evaluation from my employees. They accused me of favoritism – of liking some employees more than others, of giving those employees more leeway in their work, and of ignoring the people I wasn't close with at work.

They were right.

I was horrified, humiliated, and shocked that I'd allowed myself to drift so far from the ethics I've always held to. You need a solid, level playing field for all your employees. Not only is it the right thing to do legally, it is also the right thing to do ethically to not show favoritism at work.

After crying for about three days straight, I realized I had to change a lot of things about how I worked in order to fix the culture. The way I was currently running and managing things, I was damaging the culture with my obvious preference for certain departments (HR and marketing) and people (loud-mouthed extroverts like myself). I did not want to run a company that way, and I did not want my employees to be unhappy because they felt they weren't part of the "in crowd" that I'd inadvertently created. (Because I – and I want this to be clear – did not create that crowd on purpose. It happened because I simply wasn't being vigilant about my management. I find most favoritism develops this way – unintentionally.)

I came back to work the Monday after my rude awakening with a plan and started taking action. What I did might help you figure out if you are also showing favoritism, however subtly, in your work and if you are, how to fix it.

First, Create Distance

The very first thing I did was move my desk. I had been sitting with my marketing and HR departments, some of my favorite people in the world, and with my executive assistant, who was like a younger, funnier version of myself. That had to change. I literally picked up my desk and moved to an island in the middle of our open office next to my business partner (who was neither fun nor young), taking only my executive assistant with me. Physical distance allowed me to extricate myself from the day-long inside jokes and general silliness of those departments. They could still be silly, but I was no longer a part of it.

Then, I removed myself from their internal instant messaging channels. It was definitely more laborious to email them with everything I needed, and harder to communicate about projects, but it was also less casual; I was able to further remove myself from the inside jokes. Being slightly less available also made them more independent, which is never a bad thing.

Finally, I stopped attending any after-hours events. If it was an official company-sanctioned event, I'd show up for the first 15 minutes or so and then ghost, so the employees could cut loose without me being there. If it was an unofficial happy hour or hockey game, I simply didn't attend. Talking the next morning about what a banger a happy hour turned into or making references to the amazing plays at the game only served to alienate those who hadn't been invited or hadn't been able to attend.

As I did this, I also made sure to give my employees a reason for moving my desk. I needed to be closer to my business partner so we could collaborate more. I did not want the employees I was leaving to feel as though THEY had done something wrong, or that they were suddenly on the "outs." I had to be careful to not create a new morale-issue from, and while, fixing the existing one.

Before you think that I shut myself away in a tower because I didn't trust myself to not play favorites, however, I want to clarify that I did not wall myself off from my employees. I didn't move into an office, suddenly, and shut the door, or stop speaking to people who sat near me or came by my desk. I simply changed where I sat in the room. By moving to the center of the room, I made myself MORE available and accessible to everyone; not just those I sat close to. I've always believed in open offices, especially in small, young companies, because you need that flow of information and contact with your people.

Second, Don't Make Friends (at work)

My biggest mistake as a young business owner had been trying to be friends with my employees. I had gone through a breakup and was feeling a bit rootless and, unfortunately, turned to the people I spent most of the day with to fill that void. As the owner of a startup, my social time was extremely limited and it was difficult for me to make meaningful connections. Like most people, I spent more time around the people at my company than anyone else in my life. Unfortunately, what works well for most people – making friends with co-workers – does not apply to the boss.

By actively choosing to have closer and more meaningful relationships with my direct-reports, and not just keep them at arm's length, I was making things a lot more awkward, and truthfully more difficult, than they needed to be. It was harder to reprimand, harder to discipline, and harder to ask people to do the work they needed to do when they thought we were friends. By operating the way I had been, I had upset the power differential and created confusion about our roles inside the office by hanging out with them outside the office.

After this realization, and cutting out any after-hours non-work contact, I was able to re-establish a proper relationship with my team. When new people were hired, I was sure to keep things warm but professional. No one that I hired after that would consider me a "friend," and that's okay. I have friends outside of work, and new employees can make friends with their co-workers instead of me.

I want to be clear, though. This doesn't mean I stopped caring about my people. I still learned their kids' names, asked them about their weekends and celebrated their wins and losses (birthdays, anniversaries, etc.). There is a world of difference between a caring and connected leader, and someone you get drunk with after work. My employees still brought their new babies for me to hold, their dogs for me to cuddle, and their personal concerns for me to discuss. I was often the first person to find out when someone was getting a divorce, or having a baby because I stayed open and warm.

I think that particular balance is hard for all of us as people; but, as a boss and a leader, it is important for employees to know that you truly and genuinely care about them. It is possible for them to know that without also considering you a "friend." A large part of that balance is understanding that communication flows one way. THEY can share with you, but you can – and should – keep your personal stuff to yourself. It's like having a therapist, or a priest. You tell them all your troubles or concerns, but they don't share anything deeply personal about themselves with you.

That doesn't mean, however, that you NEVER share anything personal about yourself with your employees. I talk about my kids and my weekend, and I tell funny stories about what's happened to me. If I'm in a one-on-one with someone dealing with a big issue, I might even reference something in my personal life, or how I dealt with something similar to what they are going through; if it is appropriate. But, I don't drag my marriage issues, or my financial concerns, into conversation with them. I liken it to the difference between what you'd confess to a casual acquaintance (I spilled coffee on myself this morning, how silly!) to what you'd tell your best friend (I'm thinking about getting a divorce.)

Sharing personal information is how we make human connections with people. Oversharing deeply personal information is how we can make those around us uncomfortable.

Third, Get to Know Everyone

Once I stopped palling around with a few select people, I decided to make a better effort to get to know the employees to whom I'd clearly been giving the short shrift. Not so I could become "besties" with them, but so that I could at least try to connect with them on a human level. Part of the criticism in my 360 evaluation was that they felt ignored, sidelined, or less important. It was critical for me to begin to repair those relationships.

I knew that I would never be equally close to all my employees – there are simply some people you connect with, and others you don't, for a multitude of reasons. I had to at least try and connect with everyone. Since I wasn't "auditioning" people to be my friends anymore, it was less important that we had strong, instant connections, and more important that I simply listened, and made people feel seen. Even if someone doesn't LOVE you, they will like you a lot more if they feel as though you see them, hear them, and care about them.

To begin repairing relationships, I started doing monthly lunches where I'd go out with a group of three or four employees from different departments. They were chosen at random, and we'd go to the Chili's down the street. No agenda, just an opportunity to chat. I usually had a few questions prepped in my back pocket in case I was with a group of particularly shy or reticent employees. I also used this as an opportunity to forge stronger connections between others – these may be people who worked in different departments who might not have talked to one another on an ordinary day, but who was finally given the opportunity to learn about each other over some southwest eggrolls or fajitas.

On a daily basis, I made an effort to stop by people's desks during the week to ask how they were doing. I paid closer attention to what was going on in everyone's lives and with their families. I didn't take notes when I was talking to them, but I will admit to jotting a few things down when I got back to my desk, sometimes, so I would remember to follow up with them. If their kid, for instance, was in a play or a sport, I'd be sure to ask how rehearsals were going, or if they made it into the playoffs. It wasn't a lot – smothering them with attention would have made things even worse, and felt disingenuous – but I made a consistent effort.

Were there awkward lunches from time to time? Sure. There were times when the small talk fell flat, or people didn't want to share anything from their lives with me. There were also a couple of people who were so hurt by my previous leadership and management style that they didn't want to give me the time of day. The only thing I could do now, in the face of those situations, was to persist. I had to try again and understand that this was a situation of my own making. If it was difficult, or awkward, that was simply something I had to get through, in order to make a healthier culture at my company.

Fourth, Apply the Rules Equally

Favoritism in attention is one thing – because we are human, it is impossible to grant the exact same amount of attention to everyone in our organization, down to the minute. (This is also impossible in families, which is why I only had one kid. She can never accuse me of loving her siblings more than I love her. It's the ultimate parenting hack.) Adult humans in a professional setting also realize this. As such, they are willing to give grace to a leader who spends more time with her direct reports; as long as she is making an effort to give time to everyone else, as well.

However, favoritism in the application of rules and expectations is the single most corrosive element to culture. Having rules that don't apply to certain people because you like them, or feel uncomfortable correcting them because they are your friends, or failing to set expectations and hold people accountable to them will send everyone running for the doors. Even those to whom you are showing favoritism. Contrary to popular belief, most people don't want to work in a consequence-free environment. They want guardrails, and a way to determine if they are being successful. Without rules and expectations, no one can know either of those things.

I will give myself credit for not falling into the trap of applying rules unequally – I fired one of the most fun direct-reports I ever had because he couldn't show up to work on time. However, failing to apply rules equally to all your staff is all too common in many businesses.

The single fastest way to make everyone feel equal is to apply the rules equally to everyone. No special treatment, no making excuses for people, no exceptions "just this once." If there is a rule, it is either applied to everyone or it's gone. Period. No ifs, ands, or buts. No exceptions.

I train all my managers with this approach, and we discuss it anytime we have a situation that requires disciplinary action or a difficult conversation needs to be had. We'll talk about what the rule says, why it exists, and how we've applied it in the past. If someone advocates for an exception, we discuss what that means. (An exception means that the rule now no longer exists, and everyone has to be comfortable with that. It also means that we have to go back and look at all our previous enforcement of the rule and see if there are corrections we need to make because of earlier rule enforcement; much like vacating convictions for laws that are struck down.) My managers have been with me long enough to start this conversation themselves, and usually by the time they get to a meeting with me, we're just confirming what they already know – that we don't make exceptions.

Side note: having as few rules as necessary is a great position for company culture. Cover the big stuff, the safety stuff, and the "we'll-get-sued," stuff and then stop. People have to show up on time, get their work done on deadline, keep themselves and others safe, and not do anything outrageous enough to get the company sued. We're all adults, and should be treated as such. One of the biggest complaints people have about large corporations is that they have a rulebook about six inches thick; which makes it feel like a nanny state.

The other extreme, which is where most startups and small companies land, is to not have any rules at all, and that's just as bad. Most startup founders are exiles from corporate America or have rejected it altogether, so they start companies without any policies or rules, thinking that zero hierarchy and total freedom will inspire loyalty and creativity. Instead, the lack of structure means that the loudest voice in the room becomes the boss, and your office runs the risk of turning into the Lord of the Flies. Try to find that sweet spot between total control and total anarchy.

In addition to rules, you have to be sure that expectations are also applied equally. I don't mean that everyone has the SAME expectations, but that everyone has their own clearly-set expectations that are reviewed, evaluated, and updated regularly. "Regularly" is a term that varies, as well – for new employees, it's every ninety days or less. For seasoned veterans, you might go six months between reviews, because they are in the groove and there's no need to upset the applecart.

I've always created "clear expectations" documents for each role within my companies and made sure that all people in that role understand exactly what is expected of them; to the point of reviewing it at the time of hire or promotion and then having them sign off on it. Once those expectations are in place, though, it is equally important to hold people to those expectations consistently. If you don't, it's like telling your kids they all have to eat their vegetables before getting dessert, but then letting your favorite kid have cookies without eating his broccoli, while his siblings sit by and watch. (Or so I've heard – see above about me only having one kid.)

A handful of fair, well-thought-out rules, that are well-designed and applied equally to everyone, and that include position-specific expectations for every person will go a long way toward leveling the playing field. This will also help everyone in your organization feel respected and as though they were given the best chance for success.

Finally, Constantly Re-Evaluate

Committing to these actions once is a great start. But what makes a great leader is the ability to constantly re-evaluate your behavior to make sure you are staying true to your initial commitment of equal treatment. "Favoritism creep" is a real thing, and it is very easy to slide back into old behaviors or develop a too-friendly relationship with a charming employee. Only by stepping back regularly and critically looking at how you are spending your time, enforcing the rules, and setting expectations can you stay on track.

It is also a good idea to do regular 360-degree reviews with your direct reports and your manager, to make sure your perceptions of your behavior match up with everyone else's. We need that outside perspective to develop an awareness of our blind spots. I know I sure did.

The longer you practice these behaviors, the easier they become. You'll become a pro at developing warm, caring, arm's-length relationships with people. You'll become adept at knowing when you are being too lenient with one person or too harsh with another. You'll develop social jiu-jitsu whereby you can politely deflect an invite to a happy hour or a party without seeming standoffish. Like anything, it just takes practice.

And yes, being the boss (or the owner) can often be lonely. To fill that void, I'd suggest finding a group of your peers to rely on in a more social manner and fashion; not by turning to your employees for friendship. You'll find those relationships to be more authentic, less fraught, and more useful; and you'll preserve your company culture by doing it.

Lacy Starling

The daughter of a truck driver and a part-time librarian, Lacy Starling grew up on a farm in Northeast Ohio. In addition to working swing shift driving a truck, her dad also worked in the construction industry. Both of her parents also worked on the family farm. It was that work ethic that drove Lacy to want more than small-town life, and for her, a career as a newspaper reporter was the way to accomplish that. The world had different plans, however. As she was getting ready to graduate from college, the entire scope of print journalism was turned upside-down by the advent of the Internet and the subsequent slashing of editorial staff nationwide. Even with the distinction of Summa Cum Laude, and being named one of Scripps Top Ten journalism students in the country, she knew it would be a long road to find permanent, gainful employment at a newspaper.

Luckily, in her senior year at Kent State University, Lacy started a media marketing and web design company with two other students and discovered a talent for business management as well as a love of sales. She was so invigorated by entrepreneurship that she decided to go back to school and pursue her MBA to gain more credibility in the business world. While attending graduate school, Lacy had several marketing and management positions in Canton, Ohio; in both for-profit and nonprofit organizations. In 2007, she moved to Cincinnati and began her sales career in earnest, working in Development for the United Way of Greater Cincinnati.

Fundraising (while rewarding) wasn't exactly what she had in mind when she set out to conquer the business world. In 2009, Lacy was able to combine her knowledge of freight, gleaned from years of watching her dad earn a living driving tanker trucks, with her beliefs about how company culture should be formed and nurtured, by founding Legion Logistics in the basement of her house. She fearlessly led the company to incredible success, including several appearances on the Inc. 500/5000 list and two appearances on the list of Top 10 Fastest-Growing Women-Led Companies in the world. Individually, she was honored as a 2015 "Ernst and Young Entrepreneur of the Year" and included in the 2015 "Class of the Business Courier's Forty Under 40."

After years of helping entrepreneurs and business owners sort out their business plans and establish strategies for growth, she decided to formalize her work and build out a consulting practice. In 2019, Lacy opened her Sales and Strategy consulting firm, Starling Consulting. Her goal is to help other businesses find the same success she did, navigating the choppy waters of funding, growth, scale, and longevity.

After turning forty in the midst of the COVID-19 pandemic, Lacy decided that she needed a new direction in her life. She sold her stake in Legion in September, 2021 and left her position as

President. One month later, she became the founding President and CEO of LINK Media, a news organization covering the Northern Kentucky metro area.

Lacy always jokes that she doesn't have any hobbies, but she spends her free time mentoring students and startup business owners, guest-lecturing at local universities, speaking to women's groups, teaching sales courses to local business incubators and accelerators, and serving on local non-profit boards. Lacy lives in the Mainstrausse neighborhood of Covington, Kentucky with her husband, her daughter, and their dog, Moses.

CONNECT WITH LACY STARLING:

https://www.linkedin.com/in/lacyjstarling/

http://www.starlingconsults.com/

5.

What Kind Of Leader Are You?

Karla Lewis, Southwestern Consulting

I recently saw a coffee mug with the following quote: "Leadership is easy. It's like riding a bike, except the bike is on fire, you are on fire, everything is on fire."

How often do we approach leadership in this manner? We feel like we must fight every fire that comes our way AND lead our team to do the same thing. What would happen if we approached our leadership from a space of purpose? When is the last time you sat down with yourself and your thoughts and started to really think AND write out what your vision and purpose are as a leader? If you are leading from a space uncertainty, what will the impact of that be long-term for both yourself and your team?

People often think leading is easier than being led. If we approach leadership with this perspective, how can we positively impact people through leadership? What is your purpose and vision as a leader? If I were to ask you right now to articulate your purpose and vision as a leader, could you tell me without a second thought? Strong leaders are led by vision. They allow that vision and purpose to guide every decision they make, and every conversation they have.

Are you leading from your Vision and Purpose?

I am coaching Steve, a Real Estate Broker from Michigan; one of the things he makes sure to do is to live out his purpose when he is recruiting to grow his real estate company. He not only lives out his personal purpose, but he has also worked intentionally on his company creed and its values statements. He shares this company creed and its value with potential new recruits early when recruiting prospective new agents he is looking to recruit onto his team to ensure they understand the kind of company they are looking to partner with. Steve views recruiting as an invitation in partnering with people who can help him achieve and exceed his goals, along with how he can help them exceed theirs. It is about a win/win for both Steve and his team. This is something that he lives by inviting others into opportunity from both a personal and a professional perspective. Once he started to view recruiting from this vision – to invite others – he felt so much better about doing the activities that were required to reach his recruiting goals. Guess what started to happen? YES, that's right! Steve started inviting others into the conversation and stopped looking at recruiting as a mundane activity as a leader. To grow as a leader, Steve made the conscious decision to live into his purpose. Once he started living his own purpose and mission out each and every day, his results started to improve. The activities he employed to help him live into his purpose became fun. He loved picking up the phone and calling people to invite them into a discussion. Steve was leading with purpose. It was no longer about Steve; it was about others. It became about offering and inviting others into the opportunity that he has. He was also leading his team from the invitation. His team is strong, vision, and is successful and excited to work with Steve. His team is strong, their vision is strong, and they are successful and excited to work with Steve.

Leadership is not about doing it all ourselves. It is about learning how to get things done through and with the help of others. Once we begin to lead with a solid vision and purposeful perspective, we are able to effectively articulate that vision to others. Ultimately, this helps them create their own vision and purpose statements to guide their decision-making. When leading from this perspective, be ready for tremendous impact and change. Be ready to have your life changed – for the better – and your opportunities expanded.

It is important to understand how to create our own vision – purpose – and mission statements prior to working to create this for our companies. How can we lead from the front if we do not first understand ourselves and what drives us? I work with many individual leaders on creating their own vision – purpose – and mission statements and wanted to offer just a few questions along with the definition of what this is to help get you started along this process of creating your statements.

A vision is what you want to see yourself doing. It's what you envision seeing when you look out into the world that you engage and participate in, and contribute to.

Your purpose remains true over time. It never changes. Your purpose is your being; your why and what makes you tick. It is why you were placed on this earth and what you are meant to do, not just in your career but in your life as a whole.

Alternatively, a mission can change over time, season by season. These are the things you say "YES" to without thought.

Here are a few questions to ponder while working to create a vision – purpose – mission for yourself:

- What would I like to see happen in this world by me being in it?
- If this were to exist, what could come of it?
- What is my part in bringing that about?
- Who do I want to be in order to make this happen?
- All of this happens so that...

I am often asked what my personal vision and mission are. There has been a lot of intentionality behind creating something that speaks directly to me as both a producer and a leader. I worked with my coach to use the information I shared previously on how to create a vision and purpose statement, and am confident that my personal vision and purpose line up exactly with, not only who I am, but who I am becoming.

My vision and purpose statements are as follows:

"My vision is to leave a lasting legacy by impacting people and helping them maximize their purpose and values to glorify God."
"My purpose and the reason I exist is to be a positive difference-maker."

"My purpose and the reason I exist is to be a positive difference-maker."

I could recite that by memory because it is emblazoned onto my heart. It is the essence of who I am as a person; and therefore who I am as a leader. Am I a perfect living, breathing example of this 100% of the time? Of course not. But do I try every day, every moment, in fact, to be better than the last? When

I understand why I am leading, how I want to lead, and what drives me to be a leader, it is then that I can fully lean into meaningful and intentional leadership. This also allows me to ask the right questions and listen for the response when helping others to live out their legacy. Knowing my vision helps me to inspire others from the front and to do the things that I am leading them to do. This awareness helps me create trust with those I lead by keeping the focus on them and not myself. When I am intentionally leading from an "others" driven focus, I can help lead them to follow me by setting the right example. It is only when I am truly focused on living out and leading from my vision and purpose that I can truly be a servant leader.

Once vision and purpose have been created, we must commit to evaluating how connected we are to that. Did we just write it down and walk away from it because it was an exercise that someone told us to do in order to improve our leadership? One of the suggestions is to read aloud the vision and purpose statements daily. The reason it is important to read it aloud is that the negative voices in our heads can be very loud. However, they cannot drown out or speak over an audible voice. I have my vision and purpose statements hung in my bathroom where I read them aloud each morning. This helps me stay connected to them and to make decisions based on logic and not emotion. This helps to ensure that this is what I am feeding my mind to start my day – not all of the swirling thoughts about being a leader that tends to pop up inside my head. If I do not feed my mind the right thoughts and words, the negative, swirling thoughts are given the chance to take over.

Where will you post your vision and purpose? Who will you share it with? How will you stay connected to it? Reading a "How

To" book, listening to a podcast, and reading a blog all are great ideas to implement. In fact, these are a few of the first steps in changing behavior and in implementing new thoughts and ideas. Have you ever read something, though it was a MARVELous idea, and made the decision to act on it? Then, a few days or weeks pass. Acting on this impulse to change becomes difficult, uncomfortable, or life gets in the way. Then what? We tend to often revert to old behaviors. We go back to the things that are comfortable.

Oh, the comfort zone. The comfort zone is so lovely. It often feels like we are wrapped up in grandma's old blanket, doesn't it? It is so nice and cozy. I encourage you, right now, to STOP what you are doing. Put this book down. Close your eyes and picture yourself on a super-hot, sunny day. You are outside working, doing uncomfortable things that need to be completed. Suddenly, you look over and see a beautiful shady tree beckoning you over. You decide to stop the uncomfortable task and head over to rest under a shady tree nearby. It is so much cooler over here. The branches of the tree sway back and forth and form a nice breeze that encircles you. You start to look around. Really picture it – look around under that big shady tree in your mind's eye. What grows under a shady tree? In a comfort zone? NOTHING – nothing grows beneath the shade or in a comfort zone.

Leadership is like that vision you just created in your mind. Until we decide to act on getting comfortable with the uncomfortable in leadership, nothing will change. This is what a coach is for. All the best leaders in the world know that having a coach is the best way to create lasting and meaningful change. It is vital to have someone with an outside perspective, someone who is not

Katie Currens

Katie brings a diverse background in consulting, education, sales, and hospitality. This powerful skill set has established her philosophy that impactful organizations are rooted in building connections, igniting creativity, and meaningful celebration. Her passion for intentional people strategies in organizations is rooted in the values of company culture and guest experience she learned early in her career while working for The Walt Disney Company.

Eternal curiosity has helped Katie drive innovative initiatives focused on enhancing organizational cultures. She empowers others to take action by building an understanding of systemic barriers, showing the value of empathetic leadership, and providing engaging experiences that intentionally cultivate positive growth. Katie's work helps to empower people to put their visions into action in a way that respects the impact they have on interpersonal relationships, their organization, and their communities.

Katie is the owner of One Spark Solutions where she inspires others to find their spark through her speaking, writing, and engaging facilitation. Through self-taught and formal education, she has cultivated a motivation and appreciation for childlike wonder that has led her to exhibit what it means to be a lifelong learner.

Katie received a Bachelor's in Communication and a Master's in Education Administration from the University of Cincinnati, a Master's in Early Childhood Education from Xavier University, and several certificate courses from the University of South Florida; including Ethical and Inclusive Leadership as well as Diversity, Equity, and Inclusion in the Workplace.

In addition to her deep engagement in her own learning, she currently teaches a course on Social Justice in Educational Leadership at Miami University in Oxford, Ohio.

As much as she is a driven professional, Katie's true motivator is her family. She lives comfortably between Cincinnati and Dayton, Ohio with her husband and children: Joe, JJ, Lily, and their fur baby, Olaf. They are often running between competitive cheer, club soccer, hopping on a cruise, enjoying the Disney destinations, or embracing the stillness of "lake life." Katie is an active member of the Children's Tumor Foundation Volunteer Leadership Council where she advocates for EndNF in support of her son and other families impacted by genetic disorders. She also coaches youth recreational soccer and is host to the *One Spark Stories* Podcast.

CONNECT WITH KATIE CURRENS:

https://www.linkedin.com/in/katiecurrens/

http://onesparksolutions.com/

7.

Breathe Before You Lead

4 Steps to Incorporate Mindfulness Into Your Workday

Barbara McMahan, President of Atticus Consulting, LLC – SHRM-SCP, SPHR

Karma in business: a novel concept. Often, when we hear the word karma we associate it with people who are dedicated to a spiritual practice (think monks on a quiet retreat). However, karma can, and should, have a place in business settings as well. The concept of karma applies to a spiritual principle that implies the way we think, decide, and behave in the present moment will impact the future. What goes around comes around. Cause and effect at its finest.

We live in a VUCA world – Volatile, Uncertain, Complex, and Ambiguous. Along with that comes stress, and lots of it! According to the American Institute of Stress, an estimated 1 million people miss work every day due to stress. BusinessWire cites that one in five Americans deal with a mental health issue and Ginger, a leading on-demand mental healthcare provider, reports that 62% of employees surveyed state that they lose an hour a day of productivity due to stress. As leaders, the way we interact with others not only impacts the karma of our culture but also makes a world of difference to those we work with.[1]

Burnout is real. Never has there been a greater need for inspirational leadership at all levels of an organization. Being a leader entails much more than managing others. Whether you hold a C-suite title, have direct reports, or influence others informally, the strategies that will be outlined and described in this chapter can produce a sense of calm, collaboration, and connection in the work environment. This results in improved productivity.

As an Executive Coach and International Organizational Development Consultant, I've had the privilege of working with hundreds of leaders and their teams across the globe. I can state with confidence that these principles span boundaries. Whether we work in Dubai or Dubuque, people are human and the vast majority of us want to experience less anxiety at work, accomplish all we can, and collaborate with colleagues we respect and enjoy.

Let's dive in to explore further.

Be Mindful

Although most of us are familiar with the term mindfulness, different definitions or interpretations exist. Jon Kabat-Zinn is considered to be the founder of Mindfulness. He is a Professor Emeritus at the University of Massachusetts and is the brilliant creator of an eight-week program called "Mindfulness Based Stress Reduction" (MSBR). He describes mindfulness as "the awareness that arises through paying attention, on purpose, in the present moment, non-judgmentally."

A couple of points to emphasize here: mindfulness is about having awareness about what is happening in the current moment and noticing what is occurring without judging the value of it as positive or negative. Sounds simple, right? In reality, it takes a lot of work, energy, and repetition. This is why many people call it a mindfulness practice.

Siddhārtha Gautama conveys it beautifully in this profound quote: "Be where you are, otherwise you will miss your life." Jon Kabat Zinn's work shows the impact that mindfulness can have on stress reduction. After participants took the eight-week course, they showed an improvement in their immune system and overall physical health, resulting in less stress and anxiety overall.

Now you may be thinking, "This is all well and good, but what does this have to do with leadership?" Everything!

Just about everyone knows the phrase, "People join a company and leave a boss." Research has proven this true. A Gallup survey revealed 75% of respondents quit their jobs to "get away from their manager at some point in their career" (LinkedIn). During these turbulent and unprecedented times of a pandemic, hybrid work, and a tight labor market, it is imperative that as leaders, we proactively do all that we can to encourage a sense of belonging and engagement. AND it's the right thing to do![2]

John Sullivan, a leading HR expert on the high cost of turnover, asserts that in some cases turnover replacement costs can exceed four times an employee's salary.[3] It makes practical sense to proactively address all that is within our control to create a culture dedicated to retention.

A question I'm often asked is, "What is the distinction between mindfulness and meditation?" The two are closely intertwined but there are some nuances. Remember the definition of mindfulness, which describes focusing your attention on the present moment. Meditation allows you to do that. It provides a way of training the mind to be attuned to the present moment. Practicing meditation provides a means to achieve an increasingly mindful state.

We all have the ability to separate our thoughts and let them go if they are unproductive. I love metaphors and in his book, *Search Inside Yourself*, author Chade Meng Tan describes the mind like a snow globe, with our thoughts like the individual, tiny snowflakes. Imagine the frenzy when you shake up the globe. Now, picture the peace and tranquility that comes from letting the flakes gently settle. Meng Tan also suggests that we can picture ourselves as commuters at a subway station with our thoughts racing like the trains speeding by. It would be exhausting and impossible to rush around attempting to board each and every train. Imagine the power of using our energy in more positive ways.[4]

It is not an overstatement to say that mindfulness has changed my life. I first began meditating many years ago before I even knew what it was! I recall traveling on my first international trip to France for a work assignment with GE. I was to co-facilitate a process improvement workshop for an R&D-sponsored, cross-functional team of Europeans and Americans. As you can imagine, I was excited beyond belief. Yet, I was also pretty stressed – not knowing the language past my beginner level French, never having traveled internationally before, and anticipating the high stakes regarding the outcome of the workshop. The night we arrived, I experienced my first bout of jet lag and had difficulty sleeping. I lay wide awake in the middle of the night, staring out the window, my anxiety building as I knew I had an important week ahead. Finally, I had had enough. I decided I was going to take my mind off my thoughts and worries. So I lay back down in my warm, comfortable bed, snuggled up under my duvet cover, and envisioned my mind like a dry erase board with lots of messy writing scrawled across it. Then, in my mind's eye, I slowly and systematically wiped it clean bit by bit. Yep, that is a form of meditation. And guess what? It worked! It helped me achieve what I was in dire need of a good night's sleep.

At this point, you may be asking, "How does mindfulness apply to me as a leader?" Harvard researcher Sara Lazar discovered that mindful meditation actually changes the structure of the brain. In reference to the eight-week course mentioned earlier (MBSR), participants showed improvement in the areas of the brain associated with self-regulation. There were also decreases in brain cell volume in the amygdala, which controls anxiety, stress, and fear. All of which contribute to the development of emotional intelligence. By training our minds to pay attention to the present moment, we develop greater insight and self-control which, in turn, improves relationships in all aspects of our lives.[5]

Emotional intelligence (EI) consists of self-awareness, self-regulation, social awareness, and relationship management. By deepening our EI skills, we as leaders can remain steady under pressure, improve our ability to influence others, and cope with strained conversations more easily. TalentSmart, a leading Emotional Intelligence (EQ) provider, touts emotional intelligence is what separates top performers from the rest.

To start building our mindfulness skills, I'd like to introduce a quick, simple, and effective technique.

> *Exercise:*
> Take A Mediative Walk

To begin, dress in comfortable clothes and set aside fifteen minutes for a walk outdoors. If you have access to nature, that's preferable. Then simply pay attention to what you are seeing, hearing, and feeling. Be aware of using objectivity with no judgment attached. When thoughts enter your mind, acknowledge them and then let them go.

Let's say you decide to take a brisk walk on a cold winter's morning. As you begin, you may notice the crunch of snow beneath your feet, the warmth of the sun as it shines down, and the chill of the wind raw against your face.

That's it. That's all it takes! Very easy, and yet very powerful. The challenge is to keep your observations neutral. The American Psychological Association obtained proven results that spending more time outdoors, including urban nature, can boost our moods and sense of belonging. Moreover, experiments have shown that interacting with nature improves our cognitive ability as well. I'm sold!

As a leader, you can promote outdoor walks for your individual touchpoint meetings as a healthy strategy for improving communication with each direct report; in addition to encouraging the value of wellness, both physically, and mentally.

Use Empathy

Many people would agree that the world could use a little more kindness, so this next strategy is one that is near and dear to my heart: Bring more empathy into your day. This is a value that should never be underestimated when it comes to the workplace. According to an article by the Harvard Business Review, "practicing kindness by giving compliments and recognition has the power to transform our remote workplace."

Have fun with it! The Wall Street Journal highlighted a few creative examples from Jacob Coite, a Scheduler for Esler Cos., a window and door installation company. The WSJ cites that Coite gave out more than 2,700 compliments to colleagues in 2021. These include: "If this company was a California roll, you'd be the seaweed that holds the whole thing together." Or "Your empathy is like Kool-Aid, the way it adds flavor to a boring call." Passing out well-deserved praise is a way for you to express your own personal flair while making others feel noticed.[6]

Empathy is an extremely important aspect of mindfulness. The ability to understand the feelings of others and put yourself in their situation is absolutely vital in today's world. It may come more naturally to some, but we all have the ability to develop empathy to a greater degree. As you go through your week, I encourage you to approach each remote and on-site workplace conversation by asking yourself these 5 questions originating from Socrates:

1. Is it kind?
2. Is it true?
3. Is it necessary?
4. Does it need to be said?
5. Does it need to be said by you?

According to Forbes Magazine, 96% of employees surveyed felt that showing empathy is a critical way to improve employee retention.[7] In addition, a report from the American Psychological Association reveals that, in organizations where employees don't believe leadership is committed to their well-being, only 17% would recommend the organization as a good place to work.[8] In today's competitive labor market, reputation matters! Not only does this attract potential employees but a positive brand influences future customers and clients as well.

Kindness and empathy go hand in hand. Maya Angelou astutely stated, "People will forget what you said, people will forget what you did, but people will never forget how you made them feel." A colleague of mine shared a story that brings this point home.

Years ago, Michael worked at a large pharmaceutical company as a successful sales representative. He would travel frequently for business which, in turn, placed heavy demands on his family life. One day, upon returning home from a business trip, his wife of fifteen years filed for divorce and left him to raise their three young children on his own. Understandably, this shock devastated him. He plummeted into a deep depression and had to take a leave of absence from work. This added to his anxiety as he became fearful he was going to lose his job as a result of not being able to perform his responsibilities to his expected standard. Luckily, Michael had developed a close relationship with his leader who demonstrated not only empathy but compassion was given with a firm hand.

His leader, Scott, visited him at home while Michael was on leave in order to have a tough but necessary talk. He spoke plainly and said "Michael, the business needs you. I need you. Your children need you. I'm going to give you the time off you requested. Don't squander it." This message was given with love, respect, and concern. Michael knew that Scott had his best interest at heart and that he genuinely cared. He appreciated the candor of the conversation and the fact that Scott was willing to provide support for his recovery. Michael became motivated to get the professional help needed, took the challenging steps required, and pushed his effort into high gear. The following season he earned recognition as Rep of the Year. Although he no longer works for Scott, they are still close to this day. Taking a personal interest in your direct reports, treating each person with kindness, respect, and compassion, as well as firmness when needed, is an investment worth making.

All too often we see the antithesis of this with leaders. I will never forget the story shared by another former colleague of mine. Years ago, Linda was diagnosed with breast cancer, and rather than providing needed emotional comfort, her leader, and Executive Vice President with whom she had worked for over a decade, refused her request to leave work early one afternoon when she wasn't feeling her best. The EVP drawled, "Well it isn't like it's a matter of life or death." Linda replied, "Yes, it actually is." She left the organization soon after.

The impact we make on others through our daily interactions isn't always seen or felt immediately. But it makes a difference – I guarantee.

No matter what our baseline level of empathy is, we can always improve upon it. Here's a tangible way to improve our emotional quotient (EQ).

Exercise: Conduct A Stay Interview

For each of your direct reports (or others who you'd like to develop a closer relationship with), schedule time to learn more about their professional and personal interests. This one-on-one time allows you to express your interest in the individual as a person, and to gain a holistic perspective about their ambitions and challenges; both within a work context as well as outside of work. Sample questions include:

1. What is the most interesting part of your job?
2. What caused you to join our organization and what keeps you here?
3. What aspect of your job do you wish you could change?
4. What factors contribute to you doing your best work?
5. Outside of work, how do you like to spend your free time?

6. Where did you grow up?

Feel free to make this process your own and add questions that provide connections for you and your employees. The Gallup Q12 Engagement Survey combines the most important topics related to engagement into twelve questions. One of the most powerful indicators includes "my supervisor, or someone at work, cares about me as a person." Gallup studied over 2.7 million workers across 100,000 teams to arrive at these findings. Genuine concern counts.

Listen Fully

A proven way to demonstrate caring for others is through active listening. Although it is so important, we often take it for granted.

People spend 70-80% of their day communicating and a whopping 55% is spent actually listening. According to research by McRabian, 7% of communication is the words themselves, 38% is the tone of voice and 55% is body language.[9] Consider these statistics, especially when communicating virtually. How do you think remote communication affects this?

It's easy to see how listening fully is an important factor in building relationships. It's imperative to the process of building trust. How can you create a meaningful bond if you don't listen well?

Charlene Goeglein, VP of HR International, Acco Brands, sums up the challenge and criticality of listening when schedules get busy: "When the phone is ringing and the emails are piling up, you still owe it to that person to be present."

I recall one situation, years ago, where listening played a profound role for me. I was coaching a team of individuals who worked in Operations at a Fortune 50 company. I was confident the senior leaders and high potentials had prior access to coaches, but coaching was a new experience for many individual contributors. To this day, I remember sitting down with Natalie, a production line worker, and listening raptly as she told her story. She proudly shared how she grew up in a poor rural area and had put in the effort to work her way up to her current role. She confided in me about her relationships with siblings, as well as co-workers, and I remember thinking, "We all deserve to be listened to." This is something to consider especially on our busiest days.

I once worked with a woman, Terri, who was an amazing role model when it came to listening. This leader was nothing short of charismatic – she was able to build deep relationships at all levels of the organization. She made it a point to truly focus on whoever she was with, whether it was a Customer Service Representative or the President of the company. She tuned in and engaged like the person or people she was with were the only people who mattered at the moment. She had a great sense of humor and always carried herself with poise and grace. Her reputation as someone who served as an advocate for her team was well known throughout the organization. None of that could have been achieved without her ability to listen with empathy.

One of my clients, Bridgett McMahan, President of Besco, and electrical services contractor, shares her philosophy when she conveys, "I'm here. I'm present. I'm focused. Let's talk."

Consider the following behaviors in this listening quiz (adapted from Mindtools) and determine your top strengths and development needs. What can you do to enhance your skillset?

When Listening Do I....

Focus on speakers who don't keep up with my pace or seem uninteresting	Conduct other work simultaneously (especially when listening remotely)
Interrupt others before they finish their thoughts	Clarify for understanding before sharing my perspective
Provide supportive non-verbals	Jot down notes regarding key points
Maintain eye contact with the speaker	Keep an open mind when I find myself disagreeing
Appear to be listening via head nods or non-verbals even when my mind is elsewhere	Find a location where I can eliminate or reduce interruptions
Make judgments about the speaker if they are using different language or have an accent that is unfamiliar	Ask questions to probe deeper or confirm points

Exercise: Empathetic Listening

The Human Capital Institute designed the following exercise to promote listening for empathy. This is especially useful when your organization is experiencing a change or transition of some sort. Through continued practice, this exercise will allow you to build your capability for understanding your direct reports, setting aside your own perceptions, and viewing the situation from the individual's point of view.

To begin:

- Identify an individual who is experiencing challenges related to a change of some sort.
- Schedule a time to meet with that person in a neutral setting, or perhaps go for a walk, as I suggested earlier.
- Ask them specific questions related to what they say, think, and feel about the change identified. Practice letting them talk fully, without interruption.
- Once they have finished their thoughts, thank them and then spend a few minutes capturing your takeaways on what you heard.
- Write a summary of your findings and when you next see that individual, be sure to keep those challenges in mind.

You may want to follow up on an ongoing basis to see how they are feeling since you last communicated.

Be Yourself

In the past few years, much has been written about the importance of authenticity in leadership. Research from Forbes has found that when an organization has an authentic leader at the helm, employee engagement improves, job stress decreases, productivity skyrockets, and the overall culture improves. The Harvard Business Review found that 75% of employees want to experience more authenticity at work. Brene Brown has researched the importance of sharing vulnerability, especially as a leader, in developing trust and psychological safety among teams. Frankly, when we are all our true selves, it takes a lot less work, doesn't it?

Years ago, when I was interviewing for an internal Organization Development position for a medium-sized company, I remember...feeling very hesitant about sharing any personal details. In hindsight, my hesitancy was related to my concern that the organization wouldn't think that I would be dedicated to the role. Looking back, I realize how flawed that thinking is. I came in second for the position, and I believe my hesitancy about showing my potential future team members my whole self contributed to my runner-up status. Especially in this age of remote and hybrid work environments, people at all levels of the organization are hungry for a sense of connection and belonging. As leaders at all levels of the organization, we set the tone. Whether we have direct reports or not, when we open ourselves up and share both our successes and failures we invite team members to see our imperfections. By sharing so openly, we create a culture of mutual trust and respect. We are showing our human side, and that only helps to cultivate and create that culture of mutual trust and respect.

Years ago, when I was relatively new in my career, I participated in a team development initiative where we began the day by sharing personal aspects of our backgrounds. The team leader, who was a generally reserved, cynical guy, opened up about his difficult childhood, the challenges he had experienced growing up, and how he eventually landed where he did. The intimate glimpse he revealed was such a contrast to the gruff exterior he shared day in and day out. That dichotomy was pretty powerful.

Rather than demonstrating weakness, when we share our disappointments, failures, and lessons learned, we create a realistic, well-rounded persona that others can relate to.

I am a huge advocate of using behavioral style and personality assessments such as the MBTI, DiSC, or Thomas Kilmann Conflict Mode Instrument. This gives a team the opportunity to get vulnerable with each other in a productive way. Using an external facilitator allows you as a team leader to fully participate.

Exercise: Personal Coat of Arms

In his book Overcoming the Five Dysfunctions of a Team: A Field Guide Patrick Lencioni recommends this exercise as a way to build trust. I've used it for years and it's a tried and true method. This activity got its name by having each participant draw the shape of a crest on a piece of flip chart paper. Feel free to use any figure that works for you.

1. Each individual draws a coat of arms on a piece of flip chart paper. Next, you need to draw a vertical and horizontal line so that four boxes are created.
2. In each box, have each participant, including the leader, answer the question using pictures rather than words. This gets the creative juices going and can be a lot of fun! Questions can include:

- What was your first job?
- What are three strengths you bring to work?
- What is your biggest frustration at work?
- Where do you like to spend your time outside of work?

Feel free to include other questions here, as well. Be mindful to select ones that require only a moderate amount of personal sharing. Avoid questions like "your favorite color" or "your biggest trauma." Asking about one's favorite color provides no personal disclosure and won't bring the team members any closer. Sharing vulnerabilities is key to building trust. In addition, the workplace isn't an appropriate setting for sharing past traumas.

Once everyone has finished, have each person share their responses. Encourage others to ask questions and provide reactions. This exercise can be a lot of fun.

As we close this chapter on incorporating positive karma into your leadership style, I encourage you to pause often in order to reflect on small changes you can make that can have a large impact. You may want to use a journal to document and track your progress or capture moments of reflection. Seek out ways to incorporate calm and make sure you make space for it daily. Don't forget to take a breath. You deserve it!

Notes

1. Barnes, Victoria. "New Data from Ginger Shows Nearly 70 Percent of Workers Feel More Stressed during COVID-19 than at Any Other Point in Their Entire Professional Career." Business Wire, Ginger, 9

Apr. 2020, https://www.businesswire.com/news/home/20200409005169/en/New-Data-From-Ginger-Shows-Nearly-70-Percent-of-Workers-Feel-More-Stressed-During-COVID-19-Than-at-Any-Other-Point-in-Their-Entire-Professional-Career.

2. Gallup, Inc. "State of the Global Workplace Report." Gallup.com, Gallup INC., 20 Nov. 2021, https://www.gallup.com/workplace/349484/state-of-the-global-workplace.aspx.

3. Sullivan, John. "Why Your Employee Turnover Is Exploding – Explained by the Numbers." Dr John Sullivan, 24 June 2019, https://drjohnsullivan.com/articles/why-your-employee-turnover-is-exploding-explained-by-the-numbers/.

4. Tan, Chade-Meng. Search inside Yourself: The Unexpected Path to Achieving Success, Happiness (and World Peace). HarperOne, 2014.

5. UMass Memorial Health. "Stress Reduction." Harvard University: Stress Reduction, National Institute of Health, 2022, https://scholar.harvard.edu/sara_lazar/stress-reduction-courses.

6. Chen, Te-Ping. "Have You Praised a Colleague Today? Go on, Say Something Nice." The Wall Street Journal, Dow Jones & Company, 29 Mar. 2022, https://www.wsj.com/articles/employee-appreciation-praise-thanks-remote-work-11648562018.

7. Bryan Robinson, Ph.D. "Work Flexibility Is the Most Important Leadership Skill, According to Research." Forbes, Forbes Magazine, 3 May 2022, https://www.forbes.com/sites/bryanrobinson/2022/05/01/work-flexibility-is-the-most-important-leadership-skill-according-to-research/?sh=7b813d564a04.

8. Beheshti, Naz. "10 Timely Statistics about the Connection between Employee Engagement and Wellness." Forbes, Forbes Magazine, 27 Sept. 2019, https://www.forbes.com/sites/nazbeheshti/2019/01/16/10-timely-statistics-about-the-connection-between-employee-engagement-and-wellness/?sh=2d728e8a22a0.

9. "How Much of Communication Is Nonverbal?: Non-Verbal Communication." Working The Doors, https://www.workingthedoors.co.uk/non-verbal-communication/.

Barbara McMahan

Barbara McMahan brings over twenty-five years of experience partnering with leaders and organizations to maximize their talent and align with business strategy. Barbara specializes in building leadership capacity from emerging leaders to C-suite executives, developing effective teams, and facilitating positive change to achieve desired business results. She has a particularly tremendous passion for working with female leaders and affinity groups to promote diversity, equity, and inclusion. Barbara is certified in mindfulness and incorporates it into all aspects of her approach.

Barbara consults across multiple industries and regions of the world to provide executive coaching, team development, and training solutions. Her client list includes: Amazon, Johnson & Johnson, GE, LPGA Tour, the University of Michigan, and Columbia University. Barbara has held senior leadership roles in organizational development and human resources and has served on the adjunct faculty of the Farmer School of Business at Miami University and the University of Cincinnati. She currently serves as an Executive Coach for the Cincinnati Chamber of Commerce WE Lead Women's Leadership program.

Barbara volunteers as an Ambassador for the American Cancer Society's ResearcHERS initiative, which raises funds to promote women's research projects. She is also a Board Member of JVS Career Services, a non-profit dedicated to connecting job seekers with employers and services.

Barbara is a certified coach and holds additional certifications including the MBTI, Thomas-Kilmann Conflict Mode Instrument, Strong Interest Inventory., SPHR, and SHRM-SCP. She is a graduate of the University of Michigan with a degree in Psychology and holds a Masters in Labor and Industrial Relations from Michigan State University.

Barbara and her husband are empty nesters and live in Cincinnati with their golden retriever, Ada and their cat, Charlie.

CONNECT WITH BARBARA MCMAHAN:

https://www.linkedin.com/in/barbara-mcmahan-9980b68/

https://atticusconsultingllc.com/

8.

The Practice of Organizational Leadership

Andy Foerster, Liberty Energy

"I relieve you, sir."

Off-going Officer of the Deck: "I stand relieved."

"Attention in control – this is Lieutenant Foerster, I have the deck and the con."

And so it began. My first time solo, in complete control of a US Navy submarine hundreds of feet below the surface of the cold Atlantic with a critical nuclear reactor, a bunch of torpedoes, and maybe some nuclear weapons to round things out. At the youthful age of twenty-five, I was leading thirty-five on-watch submariners with another seventy committing their lives to us while they slept. And a nation that trusted I would not start an international incident.

I still had a lot to learn. Qualifying as Officer of the Deck – which allowed me to stand and command that watch solo – was the culmination of about seven years of intense training. That included four years at Annapolis while earning a degree in Electrical Engineering, a year and a half in nuclear power training and submarine school, and another nearly a year and a half on the Grayling undergoing a thorough qualification program. This required demonstrating detailed technical knowledge of the boat and proving that I could lead all of the normal and emergency processes that are part of one of the most complex machines ever made.

We used to say that getting qualified only proved that you were ready to start learning. There is nothing like making decisions when you are truly in charge to focus attention and hone your approach.

Thirty years of leading businesses in the private sector after I left active duty confirmed for me that the same is true in leading any organization. The mark of true successful leaders is a willingness to learn new things and become more effective every day. Leadership is a practice – just like medicine, the law, or – truthfully – any other profession.

The Navy has been developing leaders and operating unbelievably complex systems with large crews of people for centuries. The private sector has been doing the same since late in the first industrial revolution – dating to the late 1800s.

In the Navy and the successful private companies that I have worked in, I always saw two key elements that had to be present for an organization to be effective:

1. An engaged crew or workforce. Without great sailors, a submarine is just a rusting hunk of steel. Without engaged employees, a company is just a money-losing idea. Engagement never happens by accident – there must be proactive leadership at all levels of any organization.

2. A standard and continuously improved way of operating that is followed by everyone. On a submarine, the way of operating is extensively documented in everything from the Reactor Plant Manual to the Standard Operating Procedures for the ship. Well-run companies have their own business operating system, often called the "[Company] Business System" or the "[Company] Way." Many adapt best practices from each other – like the Toyota Production System or the Danaher Business System.

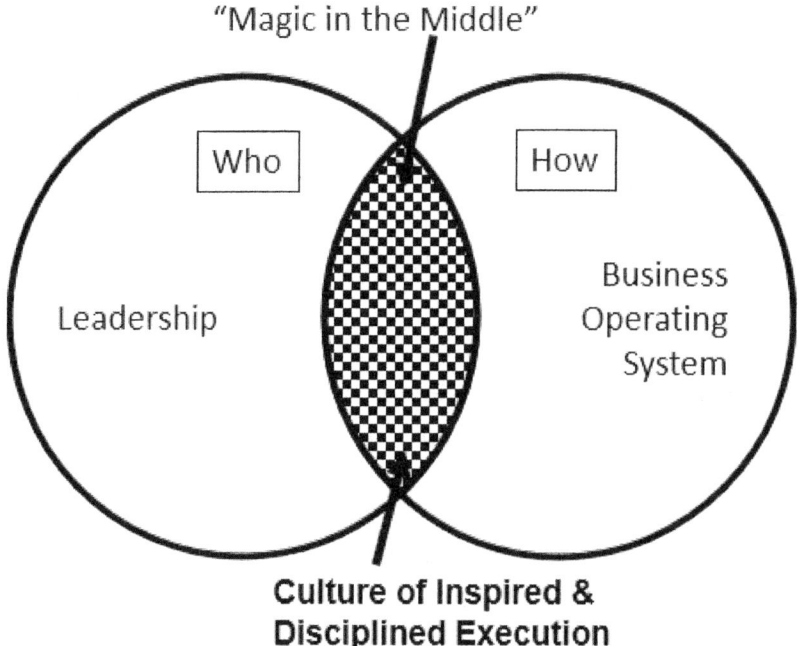

"Magic in the Middle"

- Who — Leadership
- How — Business Operating System

Culture of Inspired & Disciplined Execution
- Engaged Employees
- Predictable & Sustainable
- Highly Productive
- Great Place to Work

Want to effectively lead an organization? Put these two sides together – the people side and the system side. The magic happens when the two sides fuse together, and the people are highly effective within the system. One side is about leadership (you lead people) and one side is about management (you manage things, and the system is a thing).

The Leadership Imperative

Much of the focus in recent years has been on the system side – Lean and Six Sigma, for example. These are great tools for finding and correcting inefficiencies. Making those changes "stick" – getting people to adopt them and abandon old ways – is a leadership challenge. Let's first look at leadership, and then tie that back to the system.

Leadership is about influence. Effective leaders must align the many choices that all individuals in an organization must make every day so that they are all moving in the same direction, towards the same objective. There are many fine definitions of leadership, but all include concepts such as vision, purpose, mission, change, and moving attitudes from simple compliance to loyal cooperation.

Almost all university programs – think MBAs – focus on the management and system side of an organization. Leadership itself tends to be limited to mention in an organizational psychology course and presented in an academic fashion by someone who often has not had much personal opportunity to practice leadership outside of a classroom.

It is a problem that far too many leaders in organizations were thrust into leadership positions without adequate preparation. Often, people are promoted to lead teams – sales, engineering,

IT, service – because they proved to be great at their technical role. However, this alone does not work most of the time. Surveys have shown that only about a third of 'managers' in the United States are effectively engaging with their employees. As a result, employee engagement rates also hover in the low to mid-thirty percent range – and roughly ten to twenty percent of employees are so disengaged that they are actively undermining the organization that they work for. Of course, there is a lot of variation between companies. Some have very high engagement rates, but that means that others are abysmally low.

Is engagement important? Yes. Not surprisingly, many studies have shown the commonsense connection between happy and engaged employees and financial success. Further, the post-COVID "great resignation" has demonstrated that employees will leave for happier, more fitting-to-their-needs workplaces when they are presented with the opportunity. This can leave companies so short-staffed that they must turn away business. Note that Gallup considered an employee 'engaged' if they satisfied two simple requirements:

1. They understood how their work contributed to the purpose and mission of their organization
2. They felt that their immediate supervisor cared for them professionally

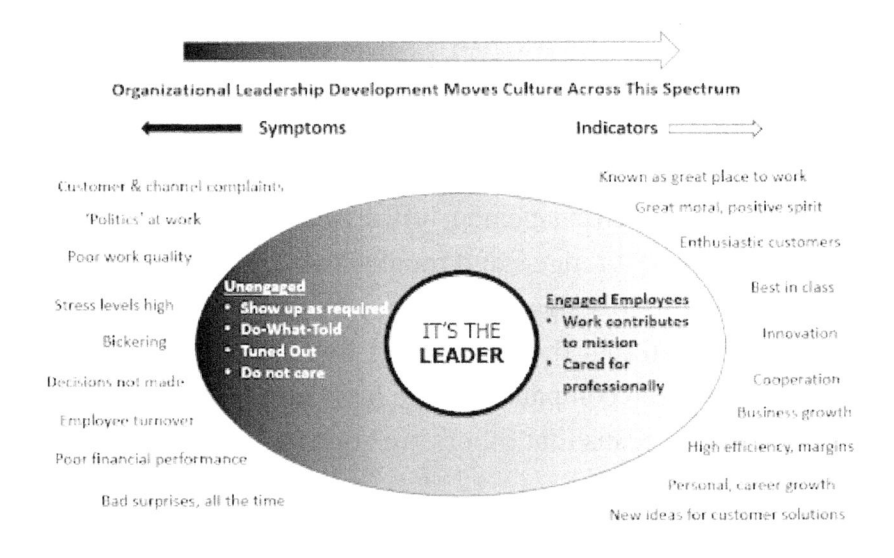

Organizational Leadership Development Moves Culture Across This Spectrum

⬅ Symptoms   Indicators ➡

Customer & channel complaints
'Politics' at work
Poor work quality
Stress levels high
Bickering
Decisions not made
Employee turnover
Poor financial performance
Bad surprises, all the time

Unengaged
- Show up as required
- Do-What-Told
- Tuned Out
- Do not care

IT'S THE LEADER

Engaged Employees
- Work contributes to mission
- Cared for professionally

Known as great place to work
Great moral, positive spirit
Enthusiastic customers
Best in class
Innovation
Cooperation
Business growth
High efficiency, margins
Personal, career growth
New ideas for customer solutions

1

The unsurprising conclusion is that leadership is important. Jim Collins made the point in his book Good to Great when he identified "Level 5 Leaders" as important to the success of an organization. However, Collins was speaking primarily of the CEO. What becomes clear from the employee engagement data is that it is, in fact, important to have effective leaders at all levels of an organization. It is not enough to have one highly regarded person at the top only.

The Wall Street Journal has reflected on the data and hypothesized that the overall dearth of leadership in US companies could be the root cause of economy-wide low growth rates.

Getting Good Leaders

There is a theory that leaders are born. Therefore, you must somehow find those leaders and hire them. That is certainly not the theory that the US Navy or military as a whole embraces. Rather than look for effective leaders, they develop effective leaders.

Much like the Navy, companies can develop good and effective leaders as well. In fact, most large and well-run companies have internal development programs. They realize that without positive leadership, they cannot operate effectively or grow. However, they are not perfect. Most people who have worked in a large organization have a horror story or two about a boss that was simply toxic – and in fact, that boss may be the reason that they left.

The initial step in creating good and effective leaders is starting with people who want to be leaders. First, people have to know that being a leader is not about status or pay raises, much less dominating others. They need to understand that leading people is first and foremost about taking care of the people who will be doing the work. That a leadership role also means they will be stepping back from doing as much of the work themselves. "The work" is most likely what they initially trained to do and have received some recognition for – whether plumbing, baking, selling, law, or medicine. For example, in large organizations that I've led, most engineers did not want to step away from the technology work that they did. Recognition of that works well for everyone – good engineers are essential, and it was critical that we set up a technical track so that they could still develop their skills, get promoted, and build a reputation. You don't want to encourage people to choose the leadership track because they see it as the only path to career growth. That would be the wrong reason for advancement, and almost certainly would result in unhappy managers with unengaged employees. Of course, not everyone who thinks they want to be a leader is cut out for a leadership role or position. There also has to be a core of humility, self-awareness, and concern for others to begin with. Senior leaders should also look for these qualities when deciding who to entrust their people.

The next step is to develop your leaders. There are certain skills that leaders must have to be effective *as* leaders. You may think that some are "natural leaders," but the reality is that they may have just picked up many of those skills from parents or coaches along the way. Developing these skills is a lifelong journey, rather than a "one and done."

A great comparison to developing these skills is learning a complex sport, such as swimming. For example, all Naval Academy graduates must be strong and confident swimmers. They will all be serving on ships, mid-ocean, in hazardous circumstances that could result in them being in the water with shipmates. Despite this, it is not uncommon for incoming Midshipmen to show up with very few swimming skills.

Instruction begins with the basics: floating and a few simple strokes, followed by practice and a review (swim across the pool), and some coaching as needed. Then, the skill development continues with more strokes, more laps in the pool, another review (longer distance in pool, more aggressive pace), and more coaching as needed. This is followed by more instruction in more skills – strokes, lifesaving, jumping – more practice, another review with higher expectations, and more coaching as needed. After four years, culminating reviews include swimming long distances fully clothed and jumping into the water from thirty feet or more. Everyone who graduates has passed these tests. Not everyone is on the swim team; that would take specialized training and some natural gifts. At the end of the day, however, everyone is effective and can be depended on to take care of their shipmates. Some choose to self-select for more advanced development in different areas, such as competitive swimming, SCUBA, and even the SEAL teams.

Leadership development should be approached the same way. It requires learning some skills, practicing those skills, performance reviews, and coaching as needed. This is done in phases over the course of a career. First-level supervisors might start by developing some self-awareness of themselves and others, and some basic communication and goal-setting skills. The next set of skills might involve understanding how to motivate and influence others and how to deal with conflict. The next round of skills could include priority setting, accountability, and coaching. Then team building, leading change, and decision making. More advanced skills then revolve around strategic execution, alignment of core values, and developing people.

Effective leaders grow to know themselves, know their people, and know their stuff. Over the course of a career, the "stuff" – or competencies – evolve as an individual moves from being a contributor through more senior leadership positions to an executive role.

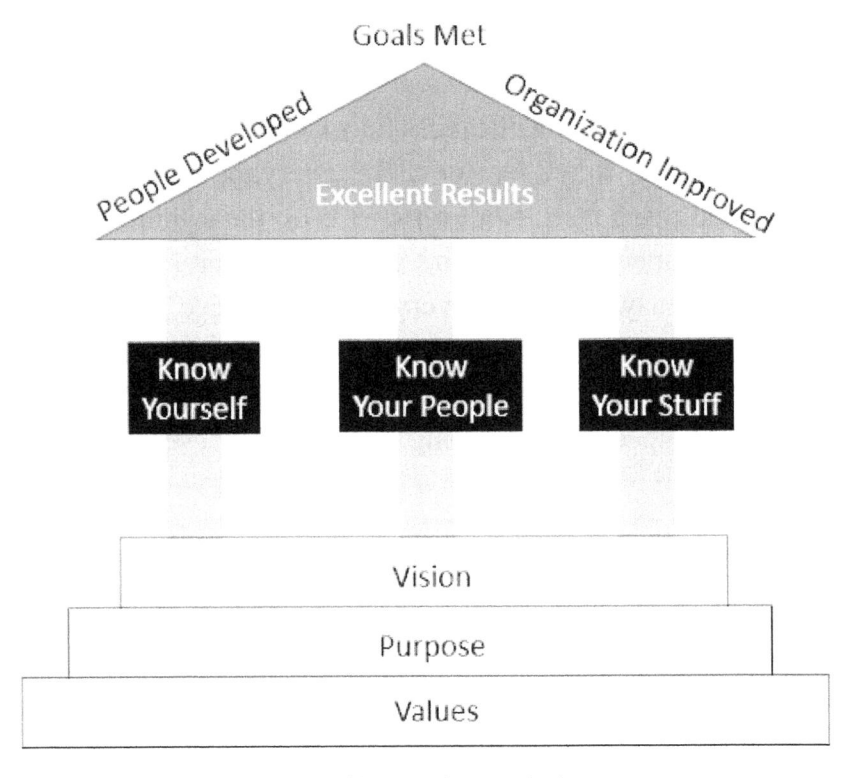

```
                    Goals Met
         People Developed    Organization Improved
                  Excellent Results

    ┌──────────┐  ┌──────────┐  ┌──────────┐
    │  Know    │  │  Know    │  │  Know    │
    │ Yourself │  │Your People│  │Your Stuff│
    └──────────┘  └──────────┘  └──────────┘

    ┌──────────────────────────────────────┐
    │              Vision                   │
    ├──────────────────────────────────────┤
    │              Purpose                  │
    ├──────────────────────────────────────┤
    │              Values                   │
    └──────────────────────────────────────┘
```

Adapted from Academy Leadership

The Navy has developed a smooth system for developing these leaders at all levels – from petty officers and chief petty officers (equivalent to supervisors and foremen in the private sectors) to junior officers, senior officers, and admirals (managers, directors, and executives in the private sector). There is no hiring talent from the outside in this world – everyone needs to start with the basics within and build their skills to rise. Over the course of a career, a significant amount of time ranging from two to six years will be spent in leadership development programs such as junior officer and department head schools, the Armed Forces Staff College, the Naval War College, and Pre-XO and Pre-CO courses. Leadership development does not happen by accident.

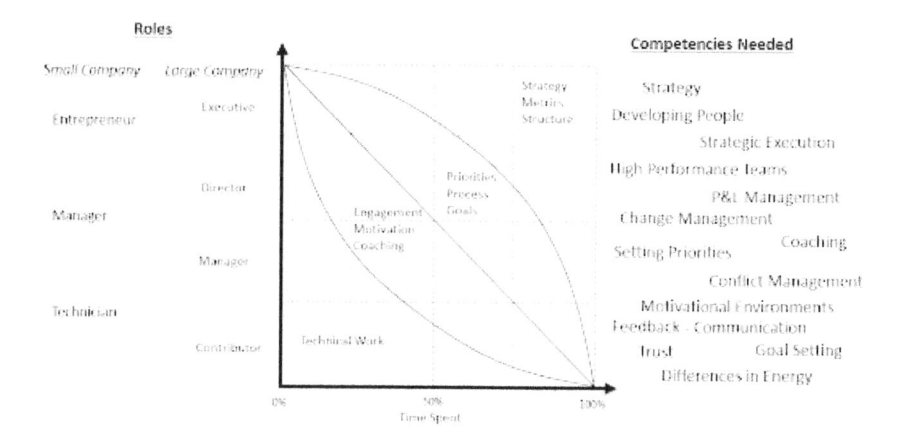

[Figure: Chart showing Roles (Small Company/Large Company) vs Time Spent (0%-100%) and Competencies Needed. Roles listed: Entrepreneur/Executive, Manager/Director, Manager, Technician/Contributor. Competencies Needed: Strategy, Developing People, Strategic Execution, High Performance Teams, P&L Management, Change Management, Coaching, Setting Priorities, Conflict Management, Motivational Environments, Feedback, Communication, Trust, Goal Setting, Differences in Energy.]

In general, the private sector is not nearly as well organized, although many well-run companies have proven that it can be done. There are several common issues for organizations:

- There is a lack of a consistent leadership development program in most companies. The first step to combating this is to become deliberate in working with and developing potential leaders. Unless a company is very large, this probably means partnering with an outside coach or firm to bring in a curriculum and help run the program.
- Leadership development is "hit or miss" with different people sent to different programs. This is certainly better than doing nothing. Incorporating some different programs also has the benefit of bringing in different views; a certain amount of variability could be desirable. However, underpinning with a consistent program helps develop a "leadership language" and consistent set of expectations among the broader leadership team.
- Routinely allowing some senior leaders to bypass portions of the leadership development process. As Elon Musk has notably pointed out, the key issue here is hiring senior

executives directly from big-name MBA programs or through consultancies. Often, people brought in this way have never had the opportunity to develop shop-floor skills in communications with everyday employees by motivating, coaching, and helping others resolve conflicts. The result too often is a highly paid executive that is great with PowerPoint in a senior leader meeting, and utterly toxic to those that report to that executive.

- Family-run businesses can have a variation of the bypassing issue described above: family members. It is crucial that all business leaders 1) understand their role as a leader and want to take on the role, and 2) are capable and developed for that role. If a young member of the family is not ready, it is better for the business and employees long-term to grow and encourage the family member into places where they fit best in the business. Stay with professionals that want to lead.

Make leadership development a deliberate part of your plan for your company and for yourself, especially if you are following the leadership track or running your own business. It must be deliberate – no one develops accidentally. Sometimes companies get lucky with a hire and wind up with an individual who has developed into an effective leader, but surveys suggest that this is not the norm.

The ideas and practices that will make an individual effective as a leader are not secret. There are a plethora of leadership books available though many repeat the same common principles. Some leadership authors are quite popular – Maxwell, Covey, Kouzes & Posner, Lencioni, Collins, and Sinek among them – and bring a unique perspective or writing style. The key is not which group of books you center on. The key is putting the concepts into practice. Practice is a lifelong pursuit. To use a different sports metaphor, think of it this way: can you read books about football – many written by people who never really played the sport – and expect to play in the Super Bowl? Or must you actually learn how to put the principles into action in your own games?

In our businesses and organizations, we are playing in our own Super Bowls every day. We need our quarterbacks and coaches playing effectively, not theorizing. For the practice of leadership, we need to cross the gap between knowing the theory of leadership and acting as effective leaders. Crossing this gap involves a practice of learning and improving every day. Every day, a leader has to reflect on what they experienced – conversations, reactions, outcomes, and more. They have to compare their actual experience to what they expected from the theories they learned from books or speakers and then think about why there may have been differences. How did their actions or understanding of the situation contribute to the outcome? Most importantly, what will they do differently next time? And then they need to commit to making that change and repeating this learning cycle. No one is ever perfect, and we all need to accept that. Through practice, it's possible to become more effective over time. The journey of Kurt Warner from undrafted college graduate to Super Bowl MVP and Hall of Fame quarterback illustrates this kind of development and is dramatized in the 2021 movie American Underdog.

Know
- Books
- Videos
- Lectures

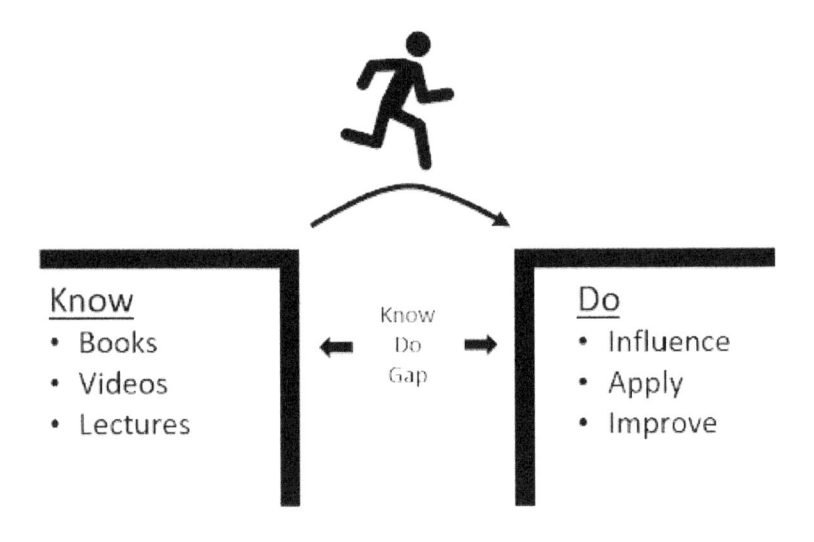

Know Do Gap

Do
- Influence
- Apply
- Improve

The Need for Systemic Operating

Many people chafe at the idea of structure. Action movies are full of heroes that run very sophisticated operations to save the world from destruction or aliens all while flying by the seat of their pants. If they don't need structure, why should you? Because that is fiction; effective leadership isn't. In reality, leaders must engage their teams in a systematic way to achieve long-term objectives.

Effective systems provide many essential benefits to all organizations of more than a few people:

- Predictability: planning provides a vision of the future. While the outcome will almost never be precisely as planned, it will usually be close; not some seemingly

random occurrence.
- Learning: good systems are all about adopting best practices. These systems provide feedback and structured adaptability to incorporate lessons learned and best-in-class processes of others.
- Consistency: everyone inside and outside of the organization will know what to expect, and who will deliver it at a certain time.
- Sustainability: the organization constantly works to develop people who are ready to step up when needed in the case of resignations or retirements. The organization is not put at risk by the absence of a few individuals.
- Delegation: people are ready and willing to accept new responsibilities. This allows for delegation to them and frees up the delegators to take on other tasks that they may be better suited to or that will help them grow.

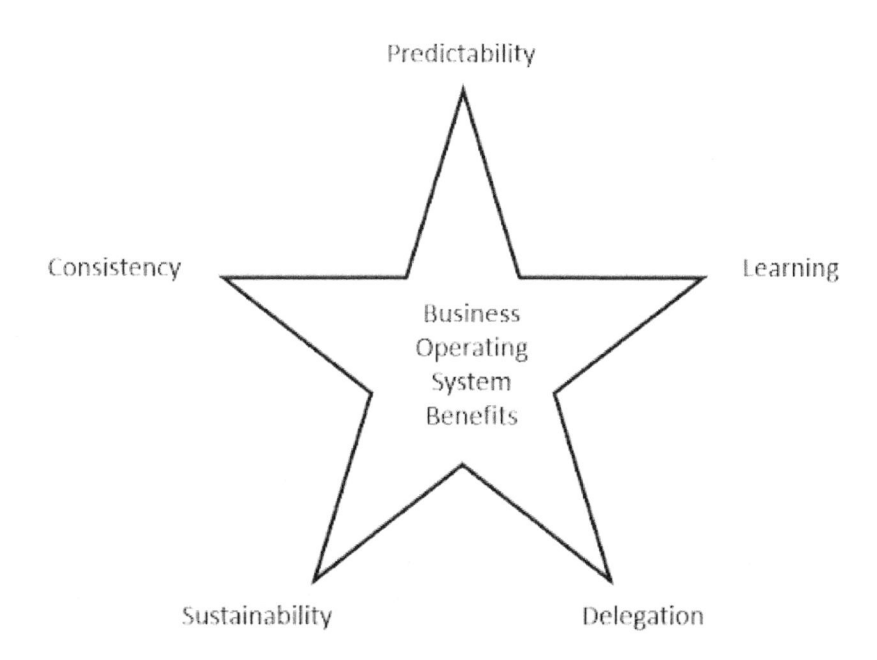

Star diagram with points labeled: Predictability (top), Learning (right), Delegation (bottom-right), Sustainability (bottom-left), Consistency (left). Center: Business Operating System Benefits.

The degree to which an organization should systemize its operation obviously depends on business size and complexity. Every large organization I have encountered, from the US Navy to Fortune 500 companies, has an extensive system that would choke a small "Mom & Pop" business. However, even Mom & Pop businesses need some degree of standardization to ensure that products and services are consistent and that taxes get paid on time.

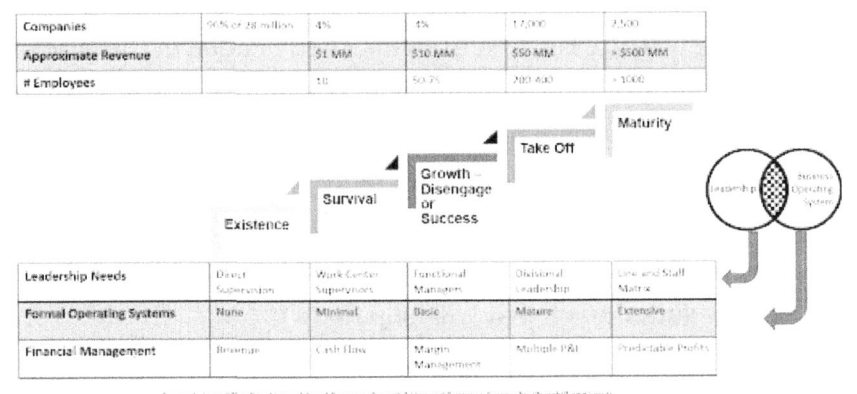

Companies	90% of 28 million	4%	1%	17,000	3,500
Approximate Revenue		$1 MM	$10 MM	$50 MM	>$500 MM
# Employees		10	50-75	200-400	>1000

Leadership Needs	Direct Supervision	Work Center Supervisors	Functional Managers	Divisional Leadership	Line and Staff Matrix
Formal Operating Systems	None	Minimal	Basic	Mature	Extensive
Financial Management	Revenue	Cash Flow	Margin Management	Multiple P&L	Predictable Profits

Stages: Existence → Survival → Growth (Disengage or Success) → Take Off → Maturity

Concepts from "The Five Stages of Small Business Growth," Harvard Business Review by Churchill and Lewis

Areas that most organizations should consider for at least some systematic attention include:

1. Strategy: Large corporations usually have an annual planning cycle that includes an extensive look at the environment they operate in and how they intend to compete in many areas. It would benefit even the Mom & Pop and 'solopreneur' to periodically write down their vision, values, core niche, big goals, and bare-bones marketing plan. Remember that strategy is as much about deciding what you will not do as well as planning what you will do. For a small business this is all best done on a single sheet of paper, and there are many templates and guides

available.
2. Organizational structure: As a business approaches twenty employees, it is past the point of one boss and everyone else is an individual contributor. In fact, it is probably past this point at about ten employees, especially if the boss ever wants to take a vacation. Many businesses make the mistake of organizing around personalities or family members rather than organizing to execute their strategy. A systematic look at organizational structure sets the stage for bringing the right people into the organization and making sure that all of the work the organization needs to do is accounted for.
3. Performance measurement: Leaders need a means of telling if they are on track or off track in meeting their goals and performance expectations. Without this, they are working in the dark. In sports, a scoreboard serves this purpose. In businesses operating with a system, scorecards are used to track results compared to a plan and prior periods. Without such a system, little more than the cash balance in the bank is tracked – and while this is a critical number, it is not a forward-looking metric. Using cash balance as a sole indicator is like trying to drive a car by looking through a peephole over the rear bumper.
4. Standardized processes: The only way to make sure that customers have a consistent experience with a company's product or service is to have standardized processes. Imagine a doughnut shop in which every baker followed their own recipe or an accounting firm in which every bookkeeper made entries the way they preferred. This would be sheer chaos, and certainly wouldn't work. Standardized processes followed by all also make it much

easier to train and onboard new people, opening a firm up to growth. Another benefit is the enhanced ability to continuously improve, as processes can be upgraded with new insights and learning and rolled out through the organization.

5. Financial acumen: Even in non-profits, there is a saying that "without margin, there is no ministry." All organizations will cease operations when they run out of money, so it is critical that companies refine their money management skills. Often this starts with tools that help sharpen the focus on cash flow. Over time, this should expand into more sophisticated ways of looking at profit and loss and improving the mix of more profitable lines or sales channels. An understanding of "bankability" and access to financing is also important.

6. Execution practices: Everyday execution of operations will make or break an organization. However, it is extremely easy to constantly get distracted by the crisis of the day or to forget to share some critical facts with the rest of the team. It is imperative that good habits reinforce the need to remember the important, not just the urgent. Using effective huddles or meetings to keep everyone aligned and on the same page is also terrifically vital. Finally, some means of tracking and resolving issues must be used in order to make sure that problems are resolved in a timely way.

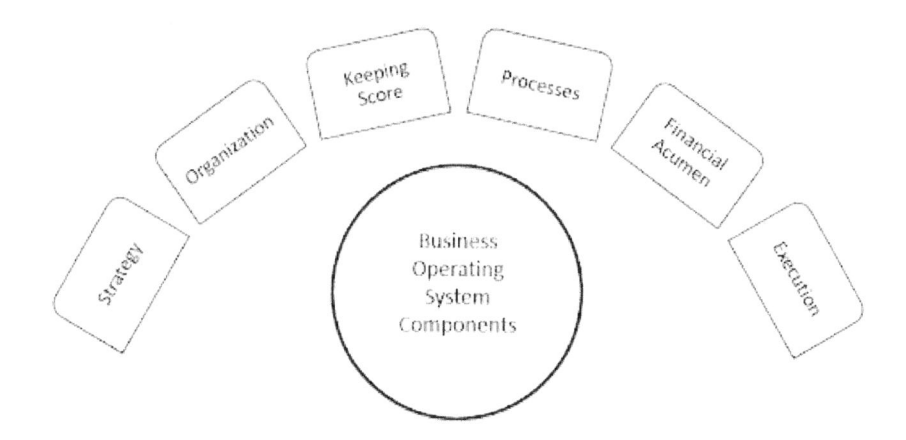

Business Operating System Components (diagram with surrounding elements: Strategy, Organization, Keeping Score, Processes, Financial Acumen, Execution)

Creating a systemic means of operation can seem daunting. However, there is no need to go from zero to a system that would work for General Motors in one step. In fact, there are many tools and templates available to help get small businesses started on the journey. Three of the most popular are: the Entrepreneur Operating System and its related book Traction, Scaling Up with its book of the same name, and the Great Game of Business. All of these systems offer free templates online that provide a format to begin the process.

Any of these systems can provide a great foundation, which can be extended over time as needed as an organization grows. Even larger companies look at the best practices of others and tend to adapt a great deal rather than create everything in their system from scratch. Larger companies tend to borrow a significant amount from well-known systems like the Toyota Production System or the Danaher System, with frequent use of tools from Six Sigma and Lean.

Large companies almost always use the services of consultants at some point to help refine and flesh out their systems. Even smaller companies often find it useful to invite an experienced outsider to help guide them through the process of starting a system. Often referred to as implementers or facilitators rather than consultants, the right person can bring in experience and perspective and help coach the company's leadership team through the process of setting up their business operating system.

The Magic in the Middle – The Practice of Organizational Leadership

Highly effective organizations bring together good leaders and good systems. One without the other is weak.

I can recall one small company that I was very familiar with. It had a highly regarded CEO who was a master of his profession and well-liked and respected by everyone who knew him. Unfortunately, his organization was chaotic to the point of driving everyone around him – employees, suppliers, and clients – to total disruption. This was leadership without an organizing system. As you can imagine, it did not survive.

It is easy to find very large companies that have well-refined business operating systems, but that at some point lost their compass of leadership. General Electric comes to mind as a recent example. It survives to this day by selling off business units, and for the first time in over a century had to bring in outside leaders to take the reins. This is a great system that lost its leadership mojo.

However, solid leaders with a right-sized business system can unleash value to customers and growth in their business. Their growth is directed and sustainable, their operations run productively and collaboratively, and they are great places to work with engaged employees that have fewer problems retaining and attracting employees.

It Begins with You

The journey to finding the "magic in the middle" begins with a commitment. Improving the internal systems of an organization and expecting leaders to grow and develop will involve change. The change will never end as long as improvements are continuous and orderly. However, it is important to keep in mind that change is initially hard for many – most – people.

Leaders in the organization must buy into and champion the change. They must set a clear vision, offer praise, maintain standards, and celebrate the wins. Most of all, they must set an example and model the adoption.

A sure way to derail the effort is for the leaders to start skipping steps or behaving as if none of the new routines apply to them. The moment that they step off the gas in their personal efforts most others can be counted on to hit the brakes.

That will leave the organization with a lot of half-implemented processes and initiatives. Slowly, most people will slip back into old habits and the organization will be left, at best, no better than it was. Even worse, many people will start to adopt a cynical "flavor of the day" attitude in regard to future initiatives.

You, as a leader, must decide that you will personally develop yourself, learn and understand the system the organization is adopting, and be a proponent of making it work. When issues come up – and they will – you must be the one to step up, seek feedback, dig into the underlying issues, and be the visible cheerleader for trying again and getting it right.

Conclusion: Taut Ship vs. Sloppy Ship

On the waterfront, you see taut ships and sloppy ships. Even in elite organizations, like the US submarine force, not all ships perform identically well. Some ships are clearly better maintained and better performers. Similarly, in every town or industry it is easy to find organizations of comparable size and line of work – yet with vastly different profitability, culture, and growth rates.

In too many cases, the crew of the sloppy ship convinces themselves that the way they are is just "the way it is." This is always a people and leadership issue, not a hull and hardware problem.

Those of us who have had the privilege of being on the hot taut ship know better. All ships face the same problems with rust, sea state, and mechanical wear. The crew of the taut ship generally makes fewer mistakes because they work in predictable and consistent ways. They learn and improve and solve small problems before they turn into major catastrophes. They encourage and motivate each other and give each other that extra bit of help at exactly the right time. They never get comfortable making excuses, but they often do find that it is easier to do something right the first time. It certainly takes less effort than doing the task over again.

Having a taut ship – or organization – starts with leaders. The leaders use a consistent operating system as a tool to create consistency, predictability, and sustainability in a continuously learning and growing organization. On that journey of improvement, every leader is improving their personal practice of engagement, influence, and motivation every day as well.

A good leader is always learning. For a good leader, every day is a chance to practice and find something better. What is stopping you from getting on the path towards a tauter organization today?

Notes

1. Clifton, Jim, and James K. Harter. It's the Manager: Moving from Boss to Coach. Gallup Press, 2020.

Andy Foerster

Andy develops leaders who deliver results at all organizational levels and helps people become more effective in their leadership roles. He does this from the perspective of someone who has been a leader at all levels, including CEO. He does not simply teach about leadership; rather he facilitates a multi-dimensional application and action program that helps leaders know themselves, know their people, and know their stuff.

Andy Foerster graduated from the US Naval Academy in 1981, spent seven years on active duty as a nuclear submarine officer, and thirty years in the private sector in several management and executive roles. Andy has a proven history of monetizing technological innovation by providing customers with high return solutions. He has organized and operated highly successful businesses as a CEO, President, CTO, and General Manager by using Internet of Things (IoT)-related technologies in industries as diverse as lighting control, uninterruptible power systems, and digital signage.

In Andy's many years of experience, he has found that successful organizations must have two things: 1) Engaged employees empowered by positive leaders, and 2) A business operating system that brings a disciplined – and continuously improved – way of execution. For Andy, "the Magic Is In The Middle," where effective leaders inspire employees to overachieve in a consistent way.

Andy has a passion for teaching and mentoring; that is a big reason for his success in the business world. From helping junior officers qualify in submarines to mentoring new General Managers in his companies as they learned to develop a value proposition and execute a strategy, Andy has always practiced leading as a coach. He now does this in affiliation with Academy Leadership, a group of graduates of Annapolis and West Point who are retired business executives and current advisors of new leaders.

Andy was President and CEO of Piller Inc. and President of Masco Technical Innovations, and CTO of LSI Industries. He was the founder of Creative Energy Control LLC, which specialized in lighting control. He held GM and senior management positions at Square D (Schneider Electric) and Eaton.

Andy earned the BSEE at the U.S. Naval Academy in Annapolis, the MBA at Marymount University, and the MSEE at George Mason University. He is a licensed Professional Engineer. He is the father of four. He is an experienced BSA Scoutmaster and is active with the youth program at his church. In his spare time, he enjoys flying (as a private pilot, instrument rated) and amateur radio (AC8WQ).

CONNECT WITH ANDY FOERSTER:

https://www.linkedin.com/in/andyfoerster/

http://www.libertyee.com/

9.

Strategy in Motion

Darcy Bien, Co-founder, Stretch Strategic Leaders

> *"Running a company without a strategy is reckless."*
>
> ~ A.G. Lafley and Roger Martin

The cost of "hoping"

One day, a message popped up on my computer screen with some warning about my printer's ink pads. I hit "ignore" in the hopes it would keep working. For three more months, every time I saw the message, I hit "ignore" again and again and kept hoping. Like magic, the printer kept working. I am a strategist by trade, so I knew this would come back to bite me. Unfortunately, picking a replacement seemed overwhelming with so many different models. So, I crossed my fingers, another very ineffective strategy!

One morning, as I was preparing for a kick-off meeting with a new client, it happened. The magic failed, the printer broke, and I was in full-throttle panic mode. I needed copies – quickly. After two hours of trying to navigate online print services (which is about as intuitive as a Chinese puzzle box), I hightailed it to an office supply store and grabbed a printer (which, of course, my husband later told me had horrible reviews and I paid too much for it!) then rushed home to complete my preparation.

As I completed the session with my client, I reflected on my printer fiasco and this Japanese proverb came to mind:

"When you're dying of thirst, it's too late to think about digging a well."

I was dying of thirst alright. My pain level was HIGH, consumed with putting out the fire. I noticed how comfortable I got at ignoring the pop-up warnings and hoping it would never happen again. I was burying my head in the sand about my printer's impending demise.

For a while, "hoping it will keep working" can hold things together, but eventually, something will break. Hope is not a strategy. I see this with my clients a lot. Until the pain from putting up with the status quo is greater than the pain of change – we simply don't act.

As a consultant who helps clients with strategic planning, I know firsthand how hard it is to change. It's as though we must be pushed into it. Statistics show proactive change rarely happens – actually less than 10% of the time. We are creatures of habit, and our brains like to follow familiar pathways – after all, most of the time, it makes life easier.

Take the Leap

During the past 20 years, I have facilitated more than 400 strategic plans with clients. Recently, my partner, Cyndi Wineinger and I created Stretch Strategic Leaders to integrate leadership, training, and strategy. The first step with potential clients is to make a case for strategy by sharing the experience of business owners who took the leap of faith!

Here are two questions you might be asked:

1. <u>Why would you proactively choose to embrace change?</u>
   ANSWER: Strategic planning manages change to avoid the pain of firefighting. When pain is avoided, fewer resources are wasted, decisions are made based on a plan, rather than reacting to stress, and the company is aligned in terms of what the strategy is and the plan for execution.
2. <u>Is the timing right for you to begin strategic planning?</u>
   ANSWER: It depends, but one thing is certain – if your business day is full of fighting tactical fires, and if you don't have time to think about where you're headed as a business, then strategic planning would be helpful for you and your leadership team.

What is Strategic Planning?

Strategic planning is far from a new concept and was formally defined as a concept by the military. The word strategy comes from the Greek στρατηγία (stratēgia) – the art of generalship.

There's no greater uncertainty than being at war. Wouldn't it be useful if you knew how to win battles when you are in a strong position, as well as when you're in a weak position? A sixth-century Chinese military strategy book, *The Art of War*, written by a general and philosopher tells you how. Many of my smaller clients are in a weak position and must find unique ways to win.

So, what does having a plan to win mean in the context of business? Just as in war, in business it's critical to win; this means finding a stronger position to overcome the competitors, even large ones. This starts with understanding your company's strengths and weaknesses, those of your competitors, and determining where and how to win. Beyond beating the competition and winning new customers, it's also knowing which battles to pick and which to walk away from. In strategy, we want to maximize the wins while managing our resources to achieve the best returns.

Look Up

Lynda Applegate compares strategy to soccer, using the phrase "look up." What does this mean? Great soccer players don't look at the ball when they're dribbling. They look up and out – constantly scanning the field, looking at the defense (the competition), and adjusting their team's strategy to win the game.

Yes, strategy means change. Markets will shift, competitors will catch up, and employees will have different needs. The mindset shift is to proactively manage the changes, staying ahead versus reacting when the pain is high. The goal is to create space and time for your businesses to look up from internal day-to-day, look out at the market and what's happening, and create a plan to win. You'll dedicate time to being curious about your market, your competition, the economy, changing technologies, and disruptive ideas.

The purpose of the strategic planning process

My clients run businesses ranging from $10 – $200 million in revenue, with 20 – 500 employees. When I survey them about their key challenges as leaders, their biggest concern (see Chart #2) is to understand the critical external changes that will impact them, including future economic conditions.

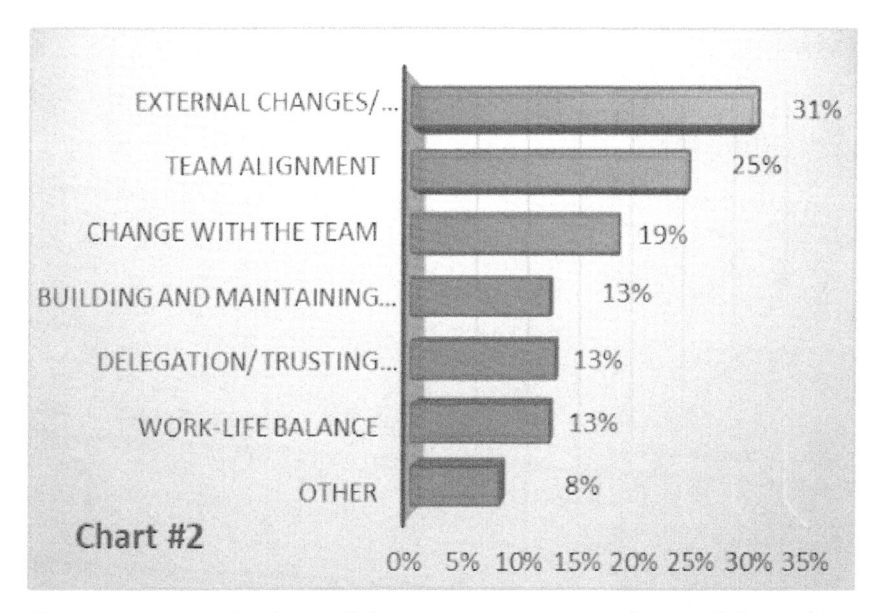

Category	Percentage
EXTERNAL CHANGES/...	31%
TEAM ALIGNMENT	25%
CHANGE WITH THE TEAM	19%
BUILDING AND MAINTAINING...	13%
DELEGATION/TRUSTING...	13%
WORK-LIFE BALANCE	13%
OTHER	8%

Chart #2

If you are a typical small business owner and spend less than 5% of your time on strategy, it is very difficult to find time

| 175

for research. It takes time to hear different opinions, share learnings, and gain alignment on key changes. Unfortunately, many just don't take the time to proactively plan for new trends or challenges. Instead, they are reactive and spend too much time "fighting the fire" of running a business. Incidentally, team alignment is the second most critical challenge for businesses.

For some clients, team-based strategic planning is the first time they have worked together and really looked up and outside of their company, engaged in conversation about key markets and competitors, and created a longer-term plan to act on new opportunities and threats.

Strategy and alignment

One of my clients, the President of a Design-Build Company, described the benefits of strategic planning.

"First, having a well-articulated strategy helps all employees have purpose in their work. If carried out properly, employee and company goals align to achieve the strategy. Prior to our company having a well-defined strategy, we had people moving in different directions pursuing opportunities that they, individually, thought were valuable, but could not get support from other functions of the organization. A well-defined and communicated strategy now ensures our people are working on a common plan."

The good news is strategic planning, done the right way, tackles many challenges companies need to address.

Strategy helps with "Alignment"

A strategy provides focus and defines choices – when to say

"yes" and when to say "no" to specific customers, products, services, initiatives, or employees; a good strategy helps you allocate resources for where you should invest to win and walk away when the investment is not worth the potential return (i.e., you will not win, or even if you do, it's not worth it). See Chart #3 for the Benefits of strategic planning based on client surveys. Having a well-communicated and unified view will result in your employees, not only supporting but, understanding why it's a "yes" or a "no."

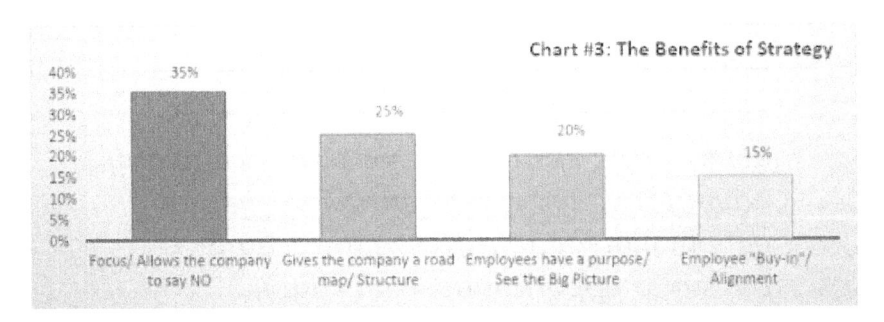

Chart #3: The Benefits of Strategy

Focus/ Allows the company to say NO	Gives the company a road map/ Structure	Employees have a purpose/ See the Big Picture	Employee "Buy-in"/ Alignment
35%	25%	20%	15%

Saying "no" doesn't come naturally, but it separates those "yes" leaders who may have grown revenue, but at the cost of lower profits, from those who said "no" to the poor opportunities.

Starve The Problems

Many companies need to free-up resources before they can focus on the opportunities.

One of my smaller service companies with less than $5 Million in revenue, started strategic planning with more than 1,500 customers! Their customers had a range of annual revenue from $500 - $15,000. The top 10% of their customers made 80% of their PROFIT. This was a very eye-opening experience. The reality is they were losing money on many of their lowest revenue customers. For two years, they had a strategic priority (also known as a focus area) called, "Starve the Problems." Before they could focus on key accounts, they had to implement pricing strategies and policy to say no to unprofitable accounts so they could say "yes" to more money!

How do you know you're ready?

Most businesses "get stuck" at certain revenue markers for their industry. Others who scale too fast, run out of cash. This is very common because the next level of growth requires proactive investment – i.e., key hires, a new technology, or a strategic shift to a new market or product. Getting off the plateau requires a growth-focused business model, cash to invest in opportunities, and an aligned organizational structure. More leaders need to become experts in their area rather than wearing multiple hats.

Laura Brunner created the Evolution of Strategic Planning model; this is a model which describes the phases that companies go through both before and after their readiness for strategic planning. As you will notice, when you start externally-based strategic planning, there is an incremental jump to a whole new level of strategic planning. Most of our clients start in Phase 1 or 2 with a goal of moving to Phase 4 over the next couple of years.

Evolution of Strategic Planning

Where is your company?

- Annual Budgets
- Functional Focus

Financial Planning — **Meet Budget**

- Multiyear Budgets
- Gap Analysis

Forecast Based Planning — **Predict the Future**

- Evaluation of Strategic Alternatives

Externally Oriented Planning — **Think Strategically**

- Thorough Situational Analysis and Competitive Assessments

- Well-Defined Strategic Framework
- Strategically Focused Organization
- Widespread Strategic Thinking Company
- Negotiation of Objectives
- Review of Progress
- Incentives
- Supportive Value System and Climate

Strategic Management — **Create the Future**

Phase 1: Meet the Budget Most of the time is spent looking in the rearview mirror at revenue, profit, and short-term planning, usually annually. When a business starts adding metrics, specifically leading indicators (pipeline, lead-time, customers, and employee satisfaction), where investment in the operation is needed to grow, they move to Phase 2.

Phase 2: Predict the Future During Phase 2, a company tends to think two to three years ahead instead of just planning for the year ahead. Leadership starts looking for the gaps in infrastructure, especially human talent, which need to be filled for growth to be sustained.

In a Phase 1 business, some critical responsibilities are still part of someone's job. For successful growth, it's essential to hire people who have the competencies and knowledge – for example, in Marketing or HR. These are roles that are not well executed by a "generalist;" they require subject-matter expertise. As an alternative to hiring, a cost-effective way to acquire this expertise is through outside support, like specialty firms, consultants, or fractional C-level people. A key outcome of a strategic planning process is to identify and prioritize what is needed from the staff to scale the business for growth.

I tend to work with companies that are ready to take that incremental leap by moving from Phase 2 to Phase 3.

Phase 3: Think Strategically It's time to switch from playing Chutes and Ladders to Chess. Phase 3 companies have a sustainable model, have done some planning (probably not formal or team-based, though), and are ready to take it to the next level. The company leaps from internal considerations to a need for "external" knowledge and understanding. Thinking strategically means looking for market opportunities and threats; it's time to examine competitors, industry research, and customer feedback to make informed decisions for the most advantageous chess moves. Because the leadership team has grown from just a few to six or eight key people, it is also critical to achieving alignment around a longer-term growth plan.

Voice from the past

Over 30 years ago, when I worked for Procter & Gamble, this quote resonated with me: "Leadership is the art of getting someone to do something you want done - because they want to do it."[12] I think about this a lot with Strategic Planning. Most times when thinking three years into the future, we know this will require change and we can see that what we are doing right now just isn't working. Remember, if you want different results, you have to

---

Phase 4: Strategic Management Strategy is now integral to the company's operations, although unlike the slog of Phase 3, the process is now energizing and engaging. Supporting the process so many times, it's my favorite moment to watch leadership teams "wake up," a concept that's explained further in the book *Alive at Work*.[1] This book cites studies indicating people are more engaged and happier at work when they are given the time to be creative and dream. Companies in Phase 4 have a solid strategic framework and widespread strategic thinking; they are fully committed to a strategic planning process, utilize proven tools, and most importantly, have a capable strategic team driving incentives and celebrations tied to the strategy.

Time to stop being reckless

The main responsibility of a leader is to proactively prepare for the future of the company. Here's the reality: it's your job as a leader to define the future. After all, if you don't, who will? We can all agree that change will happen, and we can either manage it proactively or wait until we are forced to adapt.

You'll need a learning and team mindset because the first time you commit to strategic planning, it might be uncomfortable; with practice, however, it will get better. As a first-time planner, think of strategic planning as an opportunity to listen and learn, document what's in your head, and share it with others. Then implement, keep learning, and continuously improve.

Why don't people want to change?

One of the biggest barriers to developing a strategic plan and implementing it successfully is the people part. Many years ago, I asked my organizational development partner, Cyndi Wineinger, why people who don't change don't adapt to new ideas? Her answer was simple: "They don't want to."

When she first said this, I was ready to argue. "What about the plan? What about the new reality that will require them to change? What about the...?" But, at the end of the day, she was right. People change when they really want to. This is a huge opportunity for small companies. You need to figure out why your people should want to change. Engaging them in the strategic planning process is a huge part of a successful change process.

Involving people beyond key leadership when you are developing your strategy allows them to contribute ideas to those goals and provide reasoning to support them. When they participate in the process, they feel the need and want to be involved, understand their role in making things happen, and own the outcome. Employees want to be involved, heard, and trusted.

As we know, many plans sit on the shelf because someone uninvolved in the process was handed the plan but unmotivated to act on it. It may be a great plan, but without buy-in, that's all it will be – a great piece of work, sitting on the shelf with very little impetus to make it happen.

If companies tell me they have a strategy, I ask to see it (at which point they get uncomfortable). The plan is probably in the owner's head, nowhere else. Owners tend to tell employees about it only on a need-to-know basis.

If it's not *visible* and *communicated*, it might as well be "the warranty for your chair."

So, the most significant part of becoming that strategic leader is providing the motivation for your people to embrace change with enthusiasm. That's the hardest task ahead of you.

Strategy in Motion™

Across my career, I have researched best practices and developed a strategic planning process for my clients. This is also part of the Stretch Strategic Process. I will walk you through how to use the process for yourself and your company.

Today, Strategy in Motion™ is a proven process for growing small to midsize companies. As part of the process, there are several tools to help you gather data and guide you toward your strategic plan.

My **Strategy in Motion™** process has four steps:

STRATEGY IN MOTION

① LISTEN AND LEARN
- Complete strategic assessment
- Understand stakeholder plans
- Listen to employees and customers
- Analyze external environment

② PLAN DEVELOPMENT
- Agree on current reality
- Define desired state
- Determine strategic choices
- Outline strategic priorities

③ IMPLEMENTATION
- Create scorecards and plans
- Update structure
- Link to teams
- Communicate to organization

④ STRATEGIC MANAGEMENT
- Confirm priority
- Assess quarterly
- Update annually
- Invest in training

Step 1: Listen and learn. You start the process by assessing what you already have available and determine what is necessary to research; this includes both an internal analysis with customer and employee surveys, as well as an external analysis, with industry, market, and competitor research.

Step 2: Develop the Strategic Plan. This includes your vision, core purpose, core values, and key strategic choices you want to focus on. This is an interactive process with working sessions, giving an opportunity to hear different perspectives, but then coming together behind aligned strategic priorities.

Step 3: Implementation. This is where the rubber meets the road with scorecards and action plans. Many companies become anxious when accountability increases and some even "freeze" at this stage. Our process and tools will help you over the speed bump.

Step 4: Strategic Management. The company starts to share the strategy with the organization, devolve action down through the organization, and continually assesses the effectiveness of the plan, making necessary improvements.

You stick with your plan, and you improve, but eventually, it's time to assess how it went and start over. And with any good process, it gets better with practice!

How to think about Strategic Planning?

Consider strategic planning has two parts – "Strategic" and "Planning":

1. The "Strategic" embraces what you want to achieve; or, put another way, what it means to win.
2. "Planning" is how you will close the gap between what you want to achieve and what choices you will make so that you will win.

The "What" and the "How" – sounds like a formula for sorting out any kind of life goal, and indeed it is. I'll show you how I used strategic planning in a life situation in a moment… but there's one thing missing. It's the "Who" – and I don't mean the 1960s rock band.

Jim Collins had a foundational belief that "good is the enemy of great." Lots of organizations are "good enough." They have been in business for many years, and they are surviving. Many of these are lifestyle businesses.

For me, strategic planning is deciding if you want your company to be great; for instance, "winning" a race versus just participating in the race. This is:

- <u>Being proactive</u> versus reactive.
- <u>Making choices and trade-offs</u> versus saying yes to everything.
- <u>Gaining alignment</u> versus telling people what to do.

Notice that third item – gaining alignment. This requires leadership. It is critical to first define "who" your key leaders are and then utilize a team-based process with lots of engagement in discussing "how" the company will be successful.

If you're an owner or leader who wants your company to be great, then you need to decide how to define winning. One thing is certain: strategic planning will help you define and reach greatness with the help of key leaders in the organization.

Let's talk about winning

I've worked with hundreds of companies, and they've all had their own unique definition of winning and wildly different choices. It's important to first understand how the current ownership defines winning.

First, ask the key Stakeholders (see Stakeholder Goals Tool)

When I start a strategic planning process, I work with the business owners to define what their key goals are for the company, including their vision. Here are some goals I hear over and over:

- I want more time to work "on the company" versus "in the company."
- I'd like to take a vacation and not worry or work the entire time.
- I want to be financially independent ($2M in investments and $1.5M in a 401K) and provide for my family and my employees.
- I want to retire (by the time I'm ....) and transition to my children.
- I want to take care of my employees (secure a future for them).
- I want to sell my company (for $20M) and then sit on the beach/create a non-profit/travel the world/write a book/climb Kilimanjaro/retreat to my tropical island paradise.

STRATEGY IN MOTION
LISTEN AND LEARN 🔊

STAKEHOLDER / BOARD GOALS

	BASE	+1	+2	+3	+4	+5
Sales ($M) What revenue goals do you have?						
Profit (Gross or Net Margin (%)) What profitability goals do you have?						
ROA (net profit/total assets) What business ratios are critical to you?						
Productivity (Net Sales/Employees) How does productivity need to change?						
What other goals are important to you?						
Culture						
Succession Plan / Leadership Transitions						
Operational						
Personal						

Whatever their personal vision looks like, we need to understand the owners' key goals for the company. They hold their personal goals with passion. Unfortunately many have never shared these goals with anyone else.

Business owners (which might include family members, members of the board, or investors) are key stakeholders. All of their perspectives matter. We need one aligned version of the "Stakeholder Goals" to provide the expectations for strategic planning and understand what is important to the owners.

What is winning?

So, if a vision is a long-term desired state and a goal is a way of measuring it, what is winning? Winning is setting your sights on something outside yourself, even outside your company. This should inspire the organization. Let me go back to my race analogy:

What does it mean to win a race? In a race you might want to:

- Be first, aka be a market leader.
- Be fastest in your group, aka be the most innovative in your industry.
- Be in the top 10, aka the preferred choice in your local market.

There are many ways to define winning. Some companies define winning as related to how the company is perceived in the market. For example, Regional Leader in HealthCare for our product, Leader in Customer Satisfaction (highest Net Promoter Score), Our product is the First choice. The key is measurability. How you define and measure winning will help your leaders understand the choices to make to get there.

Jim Collins didn't research large companies because he thought you had to be big to be great. He analyzed large companies because they have lots of accessible DATA, unlike private companies. Everything his research tells us is as relevant to small companies as it is to large ones. One of his best books is Beyond Entrepreneurship, with stories and best practices for how small companies successfully grow and scale.

Darcy runs a marathon

Now that you have an idea of the "why" for **Strategy in MotionTM (SIM)** process, I'd like to share a true story that offers a good example of the strategic process. So, what happened? I decided to run a marathon while in business school and it was not easy...

It's 1999 and I'm studying at Harvard Business School. My fellow students are a bunch of crazy, goal-oriented people, so it's no surprise they decide to run a marathon. Spurred on by mass frenzy, I create a personal goal to complete my first marathon with a measurable goal of finishing in less than 4 hours. My normal distance is around 6 miles, so 26.2 in 4 hours was definitely a stretch.

I was already a runner, but I needed Strategic Planning to hit my stretch goals:

Step 1 of Strategic Planning is research, feedback, and benchmarking (**SIM Step 1: Listen and Learn**). I talked to seasoned marathoners and did some research on "how to train" for a marathon. I chose the Cape Cod Marathon because the timing worked, it was close by, it was a beautiful place, and I had never been there. I also quickly realized that I need to start training to increase my mileage.

Then, I moved to **SIM Step 2: Development of Strategic Plan.** This involved assessing my current reality with a very tried-and-tested tool, SWOT Analysis.

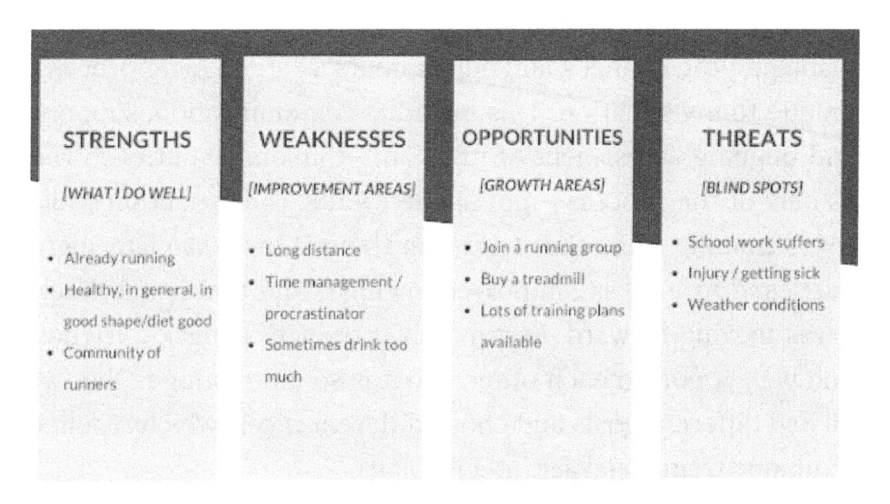

STRENGTHS	WEAKNESSES	OPPORTUNITIES	THREATS
[WHAT I DO WELL]	[IMPROVEMENT AREAS]	[GROWTH AREAS]	[BLIND SPOTS]
• Already running • Healthy, in general, in good shape/diet good • Community of runners	• Long distance • Time management / procrastinator • Sometimes drink too much	• Join a running group • Buy a treadmill • Lots of training plans available	• School work suffers • Injury / getting sick • Weather conditions

As you can imagine, my SWOT wasn't the same as my friends; specifically, my roommate, Page, who qualified to run the Boston Marathon. My strategic plan was different from Page's because it was customized for me to reach my vision and my goals. Page ran a lot faster than I did, so her training and goals were different.

Once I had my strategic plan in hand, the real work was next – **SIM Step 3: Implementation** aka the training! No one told me how hard long runs really were; they conveniently forgot to mention how much time it would take and how horrible it was to run in cold, rainy, Boston weather. I adjusted my strategic plan multiple times, as my school workload was heavy and there were other fun things I wanted to do instead. I also adjusted my training plan each week and included measuring my weekly increase in miles and time running. Did I mention how many times I fell during long runs or the time, after a long run and I was starving, I tried to make rice and forgot to put it in the water? I was struggling but kept moving forward.

The last step – **SIM Step 4: Strategic Management** – involved managing the changes and adjustments as an ongoing process, unique to my situation. This included communication, support, and ongoing assessment of my plan – thinking about each run as part of the process – not single events. Did I mention while I was training there that I gave up things I love (like late-night parties?)? As long as I improved my miles and times each week, I was moving forward. Fortunately, I trained alongside friends, and we supported each other. What is so interesting is that we all had different goals and chose different races, which resulted in unique training (aka strategic) plans.

When the time came for me to run the Cape Cod Marathon, I was scared out of my mind and felt like there was no way I would finish! Luckily, I had my support group (which I identified in Step 1 and confirmed in Step 4) cheering me on at different parts of the race – this is critical!! At about mile 14, and another hill, I was really dragging. Page jumped in the race and ran a few miles with me! Honestly, this memory still brings tears to my eyes.

It was so difficult AND so amazing. In the end, my time was 3:57 (yep, I exceeded my stretch goal by 3 minutes!). Thank goodness for my support group! It took commitment, hard work, and a little pain, but it was totally worth it.

In my marathon example, I only had to convince myself to do the training, but I needed my friends to support my choices!

For a company to develop a strategy, you need others to help, and you need to gain alignment from them and the company as a whole on what it means to win and what you want to achieve (i.e., your vision and goals).

All successful strategic processes engage the leadership, management team, team members, customers, and sometimes the entire community. The time spent gaining support pays huge dividends when it comes time to implement; you have people ready and willing to get on board.

If your company is new to strategic planning, the construction of the plan needs a foundation to be in place – some key strategic concepts:

1. Why we exist as a company (our **Purpose.**)
2. How we operate to be successful (our **Core Values.**)
3. Where we win (our **Core Focus.**)
4. What makes us different (our Brand Promise.)
5. Where we are going (our **Vision** and **Stretch Goal.**)
6. Critical areas of focus (our **Strategic Priorities.**)

The first four strategic concepts are critical to a first-time planner. A lot of time is spent defining these. After these are clearly defined, you revisit and assess how you are "living these out."

It was the vision and goal that kept me going when I ran the Cape Cod Marathon. Without those, I would have found it hard to focus on strategic priorities (my training) and the planning that followed.

Some Key Reminders

So, in practice, what is **the SIM Strategic Planning** process?

- It's a process that gets better with practice. It is not just a set of events or strategy days; it is a process that needs focus and your leadership team's commitment.
- This is a team-based process and should create more than an annual plan. I recommend planning for the next three years with clear choices and trade-offs, what is your "no" strategy.
- You will evaluate and update your plan regularly, monthly, quarterly, and annually and rebuild about every two to three years.
- The tools are proven and will work and should be customized for each company. This is critical to make it work best for your company.
- Your leadership team is critical and normally will either accelerate your plan or be the constraint. Your leader's ability to stretch will determine their ability to strategically

lead.

It typically takes three to four months to complete the "Listen and Learn and Plan" Development phase (1 and 2 of the SIM process). Then the real work begins with implementation and strategic management. That's the really fun part ●.

NOTE:

If you want to know more about the specific process, please check out our website, www.stretch-sl.com. We have articles, tools, videos and an online Strategic Bootcamp to help you take the next step.

Summary

In this chapter you:

- Looked at the cost of ignoring the warning signs, hoping, and doing the same old thing year after year. This approach only works for so long – eventually, something will break. Hope is NOT a strategy.
- Understood what strategic planning is for and how it helps you win in business. Critically, you have to look up and outside your business to gather the information you need to create a plan to win!
- Examined the phases of how companies evolve through planning; most companies start with a functional, one-year focus, and then move to an aligned multi-year strategy. You established which phase you're in and confirmed the role of leadership to move to the next level.
- Acknowledged that planning is good, AND execution

requires buy-in from your people; all your people. Implementation is the hard part of the strategy, mainly because people resist change. It's your job to help them understand the "why" and inspire them to make the change.
- Grasped the four stages of "Strategy in Motion™," the foundational process that you'll use to take your company on this strategic planning journey.
- Examined what Strategic Planning is, including vision and goals for both owners and leaders.
- Embraced the key strategic concepts that are the foundation for your Strategic Planning.

And how's my printer? The best part is the new one works better than my old one. I've learned, once again, hope is not a strategy and change is good!

Notes

1. Cable, Daniel M. Alive at Work: The Neuroscience of Helping Your People Love What They Do. Harvard Business Review Press, 2019.

Darcy Bien

Strategist Darcy Bien partners with CEOs, executives, and leadership teams to plan their organizations' futures. With nearly twenty years of experience helping hundreds of companies, her team-based approach and time-tested processes helped build her national reputation for delivering "actionable strategy." The daughter of a brilliant entrepreneur who struggled with execution may explain Darcy's bulldog tenacity among clients for doing whatever it takes to achieve successful strategic implementation.

In addition to her company, Stretch, Darcy is the Director at Partners in Change, LLC, a Cincinnati-based strategic consulting firm, and has also partnered with the Dayton-based consulting firm, Aileron, since 2010, to support strategic planning. Prior to that, she was the National Partnership Director of the National Speaking of Women's Health Foundation, where she developed new partner sales processes and created long-term partner strategies. With her expertise in strategic planning, continuous process improvement, and Total

Quality Management, Darcy co-led the Strategic Eight Planning Process with the Greater Cincinnati Chamber of Commerce for five years. She facilitated over 100 companies in their public sessions.

Darcy holds a BS in Mechanical Engineering from Georgia Institute of Technology and an MBA from Harvard Business School. Her career started at Procter & Gamble, where she spent five years cultivating operational, team development, and risk management. During graduate school, she developed a marketing strategy for Converse, Inc., Action Sports Division, utilizing consumer behavior technology and ZMET, and created several business plans. As a business solutions consultant for PRTM, she completed a process improvement sales initiative for Bayer Plastics and a supply chain management project for Johnson Wax Professional.

Recognized as one of Cincinnati's Forty under 40 and selected as an examiner for the Ohio Award for Excellence, Darcy enjoys volunteering in her spare time – she has served as the HBS alumni Club President, PTA President, and Junior Achievement Instructor. When she's not volunteering at her children's school or running her three kids to an after-school activity, she's running the trails with her dogs (who are not bulldogs). Darcy is also a Vistage member and speaker.

Background:

With expertise in strategic planning, continuous process improvement, and performance management, Darcy customizes the strategic planning process to fit her clients' needs. She implements a strategic plan and implementation process to support leadership and team development efforts.

In addition, she has developed a Strategic Bootcamp and Certification process for clients to ensure strategic execution and leads monthly webinars and Learning Forums.

Her tools are aligned with Pat Lencioni's The Advantage, Gino Wickman's, Traction, Michael Porter's Competitive Strategy, Jim Collins Good to Great and Beyond Entrepreneurship, and Kaplan and Norton's Balanced Scorecard/Strategic Maps, to name a few. She has utilized the DiSC system and Pat Lencioni's 5 Dysfunctions of a Team for team workshops.

Two books that she finds most influential in her life are *The Road Less Traveled* by Dr. M. Scott Peck and *Man's Search for Meaning* by Viktor E. Frankl.

Her recent and notable clients include:

- Al Neyer (regional D/B firm)
- Alternate Solutions Homecare (national partner for hospitals to deliver home care)
- Anchor Development (regional retail development)
- Busken Bakery (regional bakery and manufacturer)
- BDL Supply (national pallet logistics)
- Cassady Schiller (regional accounting and advisory firm)
- Chard Snyder (national third-party administrator)
- Dewey's Pizza (regional pizza restaurant)
- JBM Packaging (manufacturer of small open-ended envelopes)
- Jeff Ruby Culinary Entertainment (regional high-end dining), also serves on their Board
- Ken Neyer Plumbing (regional plumbing and HVAC)
- MadTree (regional craft brewing and taprooms)
- Matandy Steel (steel service center)

- The Perfection Group (regional mechanical and environmental systems)
- The Plus Group (national engineering, automation, and design-build firm)
- Stober Drive Inc (producer of high-quality gearboxes)
- Solid Blend Technologies (regional water management solutions)

CONNECT WITH DARCY BIEN:

https://www.linkedin.com/in/darcybien/

https://stretch-sl.com/our-team/

10.

The Growth Culture

The Mind: Brain Connection for Strategic Implementation

Cyndi Wineinger, Master Certified Professional Coach

As a leader, you're trained and accustomed to leading people. You have studied how your team members work and think. You have an innate understanding of how humble, hungry, and hardworking each person is. You can pinpoint the basic archetype of each person based on their key driving focus: results, people, analytical, or strategic. You know if their motivations are more team or individually-focused. You are that leader who has gone above and beyond to lead by understanding all you can about your team. The Mind: Brain Connection allows you to take your leadership back to understanding primitive behaviors and then gives you the power to catapult to a new level of leadership. Have you ever asked yourself what drives behaviors? What created those behaviors and how you can learn to initially skip past a lot of expensive behavioral testing and jump right to understanding people better?

Have you ever asked yourself what drives behaviors? What created those behaviors and how you can learn to initially skip past a lot of expensive behavioral testing and jump right to understanding people better? Have you stopped to think that each day you are also interacting, not just with their cognitive thinking, mind, and personality; but also with their internal primitive and reactionary brain?

Strategist Darcy Bien, and I see all the time when organizations go to implement strategic plans.

The leaders have spent four months outlining strategy and the team has rallied together and focused on competitive analysis, customer surveys, and employee feedback. The team has agreed on a three-year strategic plan and has clear strategic priorities and measurements. Everybody's minds are processing data, making decisions, and cognitively planning around why these are the right choices. Hours of thought and thoughtful, intentional consciousness have gone into the plan, and everyone is fired up and ready to go.

Leadership has followed the Stretch Strategic Leaders' Strategy in Motion process that encompasses all these strategic steps and the team believes in their people and plan.

STRATEGY *IN MOTION*

① LISTEN AND LEARN
- Complete strategic assessment
- Understand stakeholder goals
- Listen to employees and customers
- Analyze external environment

② PLAN DEVELOPMENT
- Agree on current reality
- Define desired state
- Determine strategic choices
- Outline strategic priorities

③ IMPLEMENTATION
- Create scorecards and plans
- Update structure
- Link to teams
- Communicate to organization

④ STRATEGIC MANAGEMENT
- "Look up" monthly
- Assess quarterly
- Update annually
- Invest in training

Now fast forward six months. There's a strategic review and to your surprise, many priorities have not been accomplished. Each priority leader has a valid reason why there has been no traction and no progress made. You are about ready to pull out your "unproductive stress behavior" (or what we call in the south: "to open up a can of whoop-ass") but instead, you pause and argue with yourself. You decide to continue leading with character and integrity.

You have just run into the Mind: Brain Connection. It is the power of the brain versus the power of the mind. Your team has not let you down. They have simply run up against the brain's desire and ability to hold on to the status quo.

It is time to take a solid look at how the brain works, how the brain and mind interact, and how to work with the brain to lead a powerful team to accomplish strategic results.

How the brain works

Have you ever stopped to think about the difference between the mind and the brain? What does it mean to us, as leaders, to not only understand the difference but to lead the difference?

Your brain is a wonder.

- It processes 34 gigabytes of data a day
- Transfers data at up to 268 miles per hour
- Consists of 60% fat
- Has an unlimited capacity for storage
- Contains 100,000,000,000 neurons
- Manages up to 1 quadrillion neuron connections
- Can produce 23 watts of power (power of a lightbulb)[1]

That is truly mind-blowing. Add to these basic facts the job of the brain in managing your entire body without you even having to think about it.

- Heartbeat? Check.
- Breathing? Check.
- Managing blood sugars? Check.
- Circadian Rhythm? Check.

Your brain is amazing, yet primitive at the same time. It regulates every system in the body. You can't tell yourself to stop breathing or your heart to stop pumping. People have sadly been able to live for years without any brain function in a "vegetative state." This is due to the power of the brain having the ability to keep the body alive without any cognitive, rational, controlled thinking or functioning. The brain is a powerful machine that doesn't require your decision-making for it to do its job.

On the other hand, the mind is designed to solve problems, analyze, make decisions, as well as be curious, hopeful, and imaginative. Are you seeing the difference? It's important that we do see the difference as a leader. We are up against the chemical reaction each of our team members have towards the goals that have been set and the people they serve on the team. Their minds are fully engaged in the strategic plan, but their brain is saying "not so fast." Let's explore what is happening in the Mind: Brain Connection.

Consider this primitive brain response: if a snake slithers by your feet right now, there is little chance that you won't react. Long before you have fully comprehended what is happening, you have moved into survival instinct and reaction. You didn't simply sit there and think, "Hmmm, is that snake poisonous? Can I catch it just for fun and keep it?" No. Unless you have a great deal of conditioning and training in the world of herpetology, your brain went right into the "Acute Stress Response," also known as Fight, Flight, or Freeze. In this case, research has shown that when snakes are involved, you most likely went into FLIGHT!

*(Special note: When teaching this concept, there always seems to be that one person who wants to convince me that they run towards the snake with great excitement to catch it, love it, hug it, name it, and take it home to their family. If you're that person, who has no training with snakes to fall back on as a reason that snakes are safe to you, then let me validate that this FLIGHT response is not only my opinion but a well-researched concept. Please feel free to research the instinctive Flight response by

reading super tedious research done with infants and primates to quantify and qualify the "Snake Reaction Theory." As Darcy says: "We didn't make this stuff up!"

Years ago, I took a group of some of Cincinnati's top business leaders on a mission expedition to Mamelodi, South Africa. Our goal was to understand what it would entail to start an AIDS/Hospice Center as well as support orphanages in the area. It was a truly incredible experience, and our dream came to fruition. Unfortunately, that is not the story and experience I am about to share.

At a gift shop as we traveled the area, there were rubber snakes for sale. South Africa is full of snakes and the people there are considerably more accustomed and trained to deal with them than Americans.

If you haven't traveled with a group of people on a bus for days on end, then this story may seem a bit off-kilter. However, when you are with a lot of people (mostly men) in an enclosed space daily, in a foreign country politely eating very different food (like gelatinous bone and tomato jello-y kind of food and meat you've never even met before), all while seeing people dying in horrific ways from AIDS, and then quickly switching to meeting beautiful children who have been orphaned and want hope in their lives, then you do what you do to manage the stress, smells, and freezing sleeping conditions.

I bought a rubber snake.

I can fully attest to the fact that very successful, smart, capable, and noble multimillionaire men scream when there is a snake in their bed after a long and stressful day. Even when they know that the same prank was played on someone the night before and that everyone is wide awake and waiting for them to scream, they still scream; and I didn't have to raise extra funding to cover the "Snake Reaction Theory" research.

How do reactions and habits impact how we lead?

It's been established that our innate reactions are a reality. . I'd like for you to consider that you must deal with them the same way you have to deal with our Profit and Loss Statement and our Bank Contingencies.

I want to challenge you to lead both the brain and the mind. To become a master at helping others create habits that help them to win and overcome the brain's primal reaction to stimuli.

You may be surprised to know that various researchers have estimated that up to 90% of what people do every day is from their habits and not their conscious processing.[2]

Let's go back to your team and the need for them to change their everyday habits and behaviors to accomplish what everyone agrees will be growth and success. Each person's brain wants to know that it can keep this body alive by depending on primal responses to change. Change is different and different can be dangerous! The Brain says change signals danger. Establishing new behavior(s) takes energy.

Remember:

- Brain says: "I see a snake so I run from it!"
- Mind says: "I can learn to stay calm and analyze what type of snake this is and what response is appropriate to handle it.

Team members have agreed to the new plan and really do believe in it. However, as an owner of a brain, the change involved is causing them to feel off balance. The active mind says, "Yes, let's do this" while the brain says, "Woah, what you have been doing is working just fine. My habits are good." (Even if they aren't.)

Have you ever moved to a new house and found yourself driving home at the end of the day heading straight to your old house? I have pulled into my old driveway and found myself frustratingly stabbing the garage door opener a dozen times to realize that it was not working because I no longer lived there. Whoops!

Try crossing your arms over your chest right now. Now, cross them the opposite way and observe how that feels. Think about the waste of energy it would take to begin doing that permanently. Your mind says it's not a big deal. Then, as you slip back into thinking about something else, you move your arms back to the same, old comfortable position. This is your brain saying, you are rocking my survival, habitual, comfortable habits that allow me to do our REAL work. What's the point? Don't you want to keep breathing?

Let's visit the power of habits for a minute. If the brain is telling you that familiar behaviors allow you to stay alive, then what does that teach us? That those habits matter. They provide some level of emotional safety.

It is an easy stretch to then see that habits can create happiness. The feeling of happiness comes from being able to do things well so we gain comfort and satisfaction from our accomplishments. This isn't just a mental thought; it is a chemical reaction. Seeing ourselves in a pattern comforts the brain, releasing happy chemicals of serotonin and dopamine, which increase our happiness. If you need to see the research, I suggest the *Happiness Project* or *Atomic Habits* by Rubin and Clear.

The impact of habits is easy to understand just by watching children. When a child has routine and consistent patterns, they feel safe and protected. Simple proof? Listen to a person's story who grew up in an unpredictable and unstable childhood environment and you will hear the scars and see the impact that that uncertainty has had on them as adults. Habits matter.

Here is the most impressive thing about the brain. Even bad habits are habits that give the brain safety and comfort. To change habits is to feel the pain of the mind telling the brain over and over that the new thing is going to be safe and good. Remember the key is that the brain doesn't actively think. It works to keep you alive day in and day out. The mind thinks. Your prefrontal cortex processes the decisions that talk to your limbic, instinctive brain. This is real. Your leadership is dependent on knowing the difference if you want to help people grow and reach for the best they and the team can be.

Would you like some proof? Lift your right foot up in the air. Begin rotating it clockwise and keep it moving. Now, lift your right hand in the air. Draw the number six. Did you just feel your body change directions? This is the mind/brain connection. If you do a clockwise foot movement while doing the traditional counterclockwise drawing in the air of the number six, your body will struggle. This, my Leader Friend is what your team is experiencing.

The brain wants habits and has a desire to follow a pattern. It wants a sense of safety from the comfortable old way.

Here is another example:

A friend recently walked me through her journey to eat clean and get in shape. This is a universal example when it comes to the mind/brain battle. She said the first three weeks were very hard. She craved sugar and felt anxious and, at times, angry for seemingly no reason at all. She kept working out and just pushing herself through sheer determination *alone*. After three weeks, she began to see the change in her body and experienced a much easier level of motivation. She says after about three months, the new patterns are now easy, and she craves the workout and feeling of strength in her muscles. She mentioned that now any time she eats carbs or sugars her body aches, and she has a cloudy mind.

The mind had to overcome the brain to create new habits. This is Leadership! This is what you are doing as a Leader. Casting vision, inspiring change, and working to help both the mind and the brain of your people connect, feel safe, and thus be successful.

Phillippa Lally is a health psychology researcher at University College London. In a study published in the European Journal of Social Psychology, Lally studied habits of ninety-six people over a twelve-week period.[3]

On average, she found that it takes sixty-six days before a new behavior becomes automatic. However, in Lally's complete study, IT took a range of 18-254 days for people to form a new habit. The type of change needed to form the new habit has an impact on the length of time measured.

We can easily realize how many variables there are; including the personality of a person, how entrenched the behavior is ("My family has always done it this way"), the environment surrounding the person, and motivation to change (think heart attack versus class reunion for weight loss). These all have a major impact on the amount of time it takes to create the new habit.

This is the important thing to understand: your brain wants and craves repetition, and habits. Your brain is not a thinking, problem-solving entity. That is your mind's job. When you make cognitive decisions to change, the brain fights for the energy it needs to take care of you and protect your body. Your brain wants to do its job of keeping the ship afloat and sailing. Your mind is making the decisions as the Captain of the ship. What are the directions and weather patterns I want to follow?

As you begin to move through change, your brain says, "Hey, you. I have plenty to do over here. Stay the course. Keep to the plan." Your thinking mind (you) must be sharp and strong to get your body (which is controlled by your brain) to go along with the change. When we go back to our core challenge of getting our leadership team to nail the strategic objectives we have created, the project team didn't mean to not make the changes. They just weren't prepared for how to lead the brain to get there.

Want to think through a real and disastrous example of this? Where there was a place where brains and minds coalesced resulting in the death of over 1,500 people? In one word: Titanic. The largest Ocean Liner in service at the time.

What happened? Let's start with a simple mind/brain moment. The Captain of the Titanic is told a huge iceberg is directly in front of them. It is Sunday, 14 April 1912 and Captain Edward Smith has been notified he is heading straight for an iceberg. We now know that in another 30 seconds at 23:40 the ship will be torn apart by an iceberg. His brain is on high alert. His mind is trying to make decisions. What are the odds of a thirty-second mind/brain connection when a crash into an iceberg is imminent?

Unknown to Captain Smith, the crash started well before the actual impact at 23:40. The Titanic has received six radio messages of an unusually high occurrence of icebergs and ice floats in the area. Why hasn't Captain Smith been notified? The ship's radio operators are not his crew. They are employees of the Marconi Company who have the key strategic goal of being the pioneer of wireless long-distance communication and mass media broadcasting. They are focused on building a global communications company. There is one goal for the operators. They must deliver long-distance messages to prove the viability of the company's ability to transmit global communications. Icebergs are not a priority.

Think for a moment if that was you. You get to sail on the Titanic. If you do your job well, you will be the first to send messages from the most prestigious ship ever set sail to people on land and then across the globe. Your family, friends, colleagues, and the world know that you are about to break the barriers of anything ever done before in the world of communication.

Your radios are down. Crickets. You have some of the most important people in the world on board. You have been selected by your company's leadership as the most capable person to set a new standard in the world. And your radios are down.

Your mind is reeling. Your heart is pounding. Your body has you staying alive with adrenaline and survival instincts. There is nowhere to run, there is no place to hide, you must fight your way through it.

You get the sixth call from another ship reporting ice in the area. Do they not understand what is happening here? You are in the middle of changing the world. The ship is invincible and all you must do is let important people send messages to important people and you will never have to worry about providing for your family again. You will be famous. You have trained to send messages. No one helped your mind think about the fact that you are also the main conduit for emergency broadcast messages.

Broken equipment has you on high-adrenaline-alert. You are in survival mode for what you have been trained to do; you are doing it. If you don't, then are you going to see the look of failure and shame in your family's eyes?

When the final of the six messages calling out the danger ahead for the Titanic now traveling at almost full speed of twenty-two knots or twenty-five miles per hour comes in at 22:30 from operator Cyril Evans of the nearby ship the Californian, the radio operator, Jack Phillips failed to grasp the significance and impact of the message. His mind was in survival mode. He had been trained on the importance of getting messages relayed for passengers: not go keep the Titanic safe. His brain did not engage with the measure and impact of the issue.

Mr. Phillips cut off the message and signaled back "Shut up! Shut up! I'm working Cape Race."

Cape Race was the Newfoundland-based ground receiver for the messages being sent by the rich and famous people on board the Titanic. His mind: brain connection was in full play. The goal at the forefront of his mind: is to be a part of the success of the Marconi Company.

So, what happened?

Mr. Phillips makes a call to the quarterdeck to alert the ship to avoid the iceberg. From there, many were involved in trying to save the Titanic...a Quartermaster, a Second Officer, and a First Officer. The list goes on as each man tried to do what he believed to be the right thing in those moments. There was little these highly trained men could do because of the delay of the information.

We can only hope to learn from events like the sinking of the Titanic. At a minimum, it shows that what the brain and the mind prepare for is what they see. If you train your mind to see success in transmitting out messages, then one will do that to be safe. If you train your mind to understand that icebergs can equal death, then one will process that accordingly to be safe. If you hope that your brain will always accomplish the vision and that your brain is smart enough to understand six calls about an iceberg? We will not accomplish our vision. We must connect the mind with the brain.

The mind: brain connection.

Let's imagine that you are on vacation. Every day you look out across a beautiful island. Every morning, you tell yourself, "This is the day. I am going to swim to that island and check it out. I will be the great explorer who pushes for great accomplishments even while on vacation." Each day you get stronger and closer to the island. You imagine yourself walking out of the water and up to the shore. You are Serena Williams winning the 24th Grand Slam. You are invincible.

It is the final day of your vacation and you have decided that nothing is going to stop you.

You dive into the water. You are strong and driven. You swim. You look up to judge the distance and while you feel yourself getting closer, it is hard to tell just how close you actually are.

Then it occurs to you. "I'm going to have to swim back from my island once I get there. Is this really my goal? Is this truly worth it? What if I can't make it back? Who is going to find me? Will I have enough energy to load the minivan and drive everyone back home? Is my life insurance paid? I have that project at work due...and I can't let the team down..."

Your mind says "YES! SWIM! I trained for this all week. I can do this." Your body says "maybe." Then your survival instincts kick into gear. The brain says "WAIT!" The mind says "GO!" The brain says "Danger!" The mind says "KICK harder!" The body feels the adrenaline kick into high gear. This is the battle of the brain and mind.

At this moment, if you have not trained your mind and brain's control of the body to handle the adrenaline that comes with change. You will not be able to push through this internal struggle. You have just experienced cognitive dissonance. This is the state of being stuck; the state of: "protect, survive, fight, flight, or freeze."

Here is how Google defines it:

Cognitive Dissonance is the perception of contradictory information. Relevant items of information include a person's actions, feelings, ideas, beliefs, values, and things in the environment. Cognitive dissonance is typically experienced as psychological stress when persons participate in an action that goes against one or more of those things.

According to this theory, when two actions or ideas are not psychologically consistent with each other, people do all in their power to change them until they become consistent

The discomfort is triggered by the person's belief clashing with new information perceived, wherein the individual tries to find a way to resolve the contradiction to reduce their discomfort [4]

When the mind and brain aren't in sync, this is what happens:

"MESSY" MIDDLE

Why don't we accomplish everything we set our minds to do? If we really truly want something, then why don't we just manifest, or muscle it, into being? Or why don't we simply put a plan on paper and then do it step-by-step? Because we experience the "Acute Stress Response" when our brain perceives danger and overrides our thinking mind and the cognitive brain goes into protection mode.

Think about how the definition of cognitive dissonance plays out for us. It is the space where your mind wants something, but your brain contradicts what you think, believe, or value and is causing you psychological stress.

- "The promotion is incredible, but I don't want to travel and miss out on my family events. The money and opportunity are amazing, but at what price for my family?"
- "I'm a recruiter and required to tell people they can earn $50-89k per year. They would have to be here 30 years to reach $89k. My value system doesn't deem this, to be honest, but it is what I have to say."

We have a myriad of reasons why our plans and goals don't get accomplished. At the heart of it, you may be surprised to know what the reason is for you.

You may be asking yourself right now if you believe this to be true. Challenge yourself to think back to any goal you've set for yourself in your life that you haven't yet accomplished. What happened? Did a plane crash into your house or did the dog eat your homework? Why weren't you successful?

- Not enough resources?
- Too much risk?
- Not enough time?
- A bad plan?

Yes, all of these are real and very valid reasons that your plan went awry. If you really had to track down solutions to any of those issues or reasons, could you possibly see that all doors of possibility lead back to you? Why have other people pushed forward and yet you have not accomplished your goal?

Not enough resources? Bernie Bergan of Norway became a licensed driver of an 18-wheeler in 2018. Why is that any big deal? Bernie is a paraplegic. I would call that the ultimate lack of resources when it comes to driving up to 80,000 pounds. Yet, he figured out a way. He has special lifts, special handles, and systems for unloading the trailer completely on his own.

I once attempted to drive a cab of an 18-wheeler, and it was impossibly difficult. My dad had purchased one for his business and he knew I loved a challenge. I think he regretted letting me drive it (as he did for several other motorized vehicles in his life). I felt like every part of my physical body was working to try and keep it on the road. I can't imagine doing that with only the upper portion of my body at my immediate disposal. Mr. Bergan didn't let his mind hold him back. He helped his mind and brain work together.

Too much risk? Whether or not you are a fan, Jeff Bezos is an incredible story. He didn't have to take a risk. A graduate of Princeton University, he had a high-paying job on Wall Street as the senior vice president of the hedge fund D.E. Shaw & Co. Bezos has been quoted saying the position was not what he dreamed of when he saw himself at 90 years old. In 1994, he risked it all by leaving his job to start Amazon. Think about this: Amazon was only an online bookstore being run out of his garage at the time.

People like Bezos have a high tolerance for risk, but clearly, he knows how to manage his Mind: Brain Connection. Today, he also heads the spaceflight company Blue Origin, and is the wealthiest man in the world, with a net worth of over $160 billion.

Not enough time? Who can't pass up an opportunity to go back to the movie Apollo 13? Talk about not enough time to solve a complicated life or death problem. The movie depicts the 1994 book *Lost Moon: The Perilous Voyage of Apollo 13*, by astronaut Jim Lovell and Jeffrey Kluger.[5] As Apollo 13 loses electricity, the required oxygen, and energy to get the men and mission home alive, Tom Hanks, oh I mean Jim Lovell, is at his best. THIS is a time problem. Not enough power, oxygen, time, or resources to live? Yet, they pushed past all fear, used their highly trained brains, and found a solution to come home. If you haven't watched the film, stream it. You won't be disappointed.

I try to imagine myself in that situation. The closest I can come to a similar scenario is while scuba diving in the Bahamas, a huge green Moray Eel swam right toward me. At the last second, he swam over my right shoulder barely missing my mask by inches, not feet. I sucked more air out of my tank than I had for the previous 30 minutes of diving. When I think about Apollo 13, I can't imagine being in space and knowing that I absolutely had to stay calm, figure out the solution, and not suck up all the remaining air. The astronauts had trained for this moment. Discipline. Practice. Knowledge. This is the stuff of leadership.

Can you see how each of these stories represents the mind: brain connection? Can you reason that accomplishing your goals and dreams may have nothing to do with being limited in resources, risks, time, etc.? Can you see the power of leading your team to form new habits, accomplish new dreams, and feel safe in the process? I see it for you.

You GOT this. The Leadership of Winners

Let's do a quick review of what we now know.

The brain is fighting to keep your body alive at any cost. Your mind is helping you learn, problem solve and tackle dreams, goals, and aspirations. Your role as a leader is to help your team connect the mind and brain to achieve goals, dreams, and strategic initiatives, and to experience the joy and satisfaction of winning.

I'm going to give you a quick cheat sheet here. You are going to watch your team run to three responses when you initiate change.

3 CHOICES

FREEZE — "Frozen Man"

FLIGHT — "Went to Florida"

FIGHT — "Prepare to Win"

Scientifically, your brain will be on guard to protect your body. When it perceives danger, it is going to tell the adrenal glands to release adrenaline. Those darn little "stress hormone" producers sit right above your kidneys. Why is that important? Because they can send chemicals to your body before the mind even gets wind of it. Suddenly, your major muscle groups are full of powerhouse drugs. Your heart gets the message to rev up into overdrive. The mind gets flooded with adrenaline which is basically what I call its "stupid chemical." Your brain shuts everything not needed down so the muscles and heart can protect you.

At this moment your body decides to Fight: get aggressive, hulk up, and push.

Or it decides to Flight: get the hell outta here, run; at least run faster than the guy behind you if the bear is chasing you.

| 223

Or Freeze: stand very still. Don't move or the predator might see you. This is the moment when it feels like the sound of your heartbeat in your ears is loud enough to wake the world.

This is what your team is experiencing; at least at some level. The pain of staying the same must be more than the pain of change...but who knew that the entire body is working on staying the same and avoiding change? Who knew? And you must lead through it.

Now you do. Even you are going to have a moment when you feel that leaving on a permanent vacation to Florida is better than this. You may want to lead this change more than anything, but watching your trusted team go through FFF is a lot to manage.

Our Stretch Strategic Leadership Process is designed to help you integrate strategy and leadership skills. If you allow your team to rationally design a process and then expect them to move through to the new habits needed for execution without support and training, you are wishing upon a star.

Here is the way to lead through this change.

Understand how to be a Healthy Leader.

THE STRETCH HEALTHY LEADER EQUATION

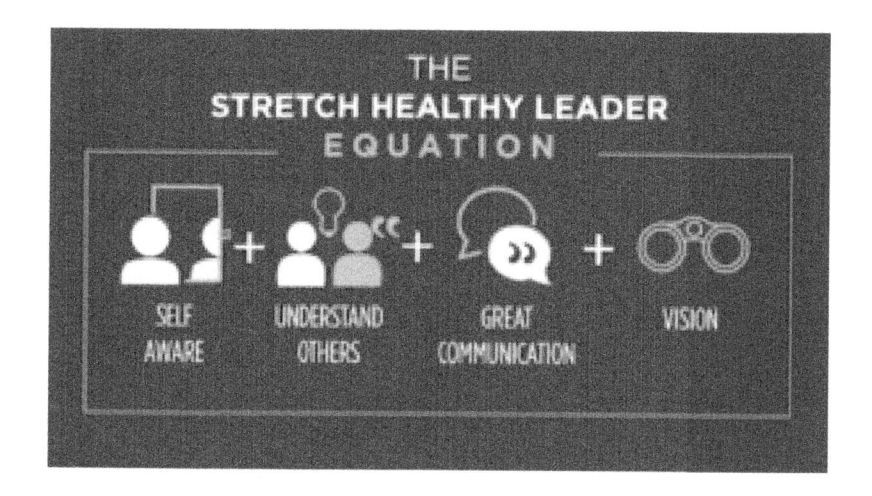

SELF AWARE + UNDERSTAND OTHERS + GREAT COMMUNICATION + VISION

Grow your team. You must practice and practice how to respond to the snake until you succeed.

Lead by creating a Growth Culture.

HEALTHY LEADERS
Assess & Train
Self-aware
Understand Others
Great Communicator
Visionary

WINNING STRATEGIES
Train & Plan
Listen & Learn
Current Reality
Desired State
Strategic Choices

HIGH PERFORMANCE TEAMS
Implement & Expand
Role Clarity
Culture Activators
Dynamic Teams
Change Management

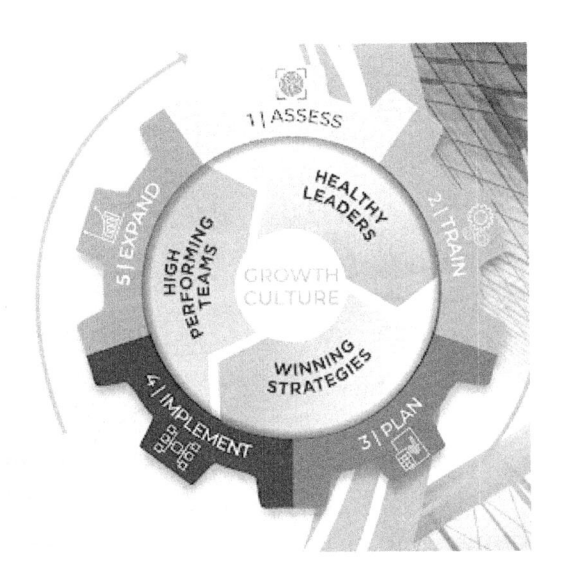

Therefore, strategy always requires the balance of impacting the brain and building trust in teamwork at the same time. A strategy plan without impacting behavior, safety, and trust with your team are just nice to know.

Leaders lead brains AND minds to new levels of performance. This is the leadership knowledge that will take you to new heights. The Mind: Brain Connection existed long before any behavioral assessment helped you to lead your team. To learn more, let's talk about how Strategy creates the perfect space for new habits and winning.

Notes

1. Northwestern Medicine. "11 Fun Facts about Your Brain." Northwestern Medicine, Oct. 2019, https://www.nm.org/healthbeat/healthy-tips/11-fun-facts-about-your-brain.
2. Walesh, Stuart G. "Using the Power of Habits to Work Smarter."

Helpingyouengineeryourfuture.com, Catalyst Marketing, 2017, http://www.helpingyouengineeryourfuture.com/habits-work-smarter.htm.

3. Lalley, Phillippa. "How Are Habits Formed: Modelling Habit Formation ... - Wiley Online Library." Wiley Online Library, European Journal of Social Psychology, 16 July 2009, https://onlinelibrary.wiley.com/doi/abs/10.1002/ejsp.674.
4. Festinger, L. (1957). A Theory of Cognitive Dissonance. California: Stanford University Press.
5. Lovell, Jim, and Jeffrey Kluger. Lost Moon: The Perilous Voyage of Apollo 13. Houghton Mifflin, 1994.

Cyndi Wineinger

Cyndi is passionate about coaching people as well as organizations so they can operate from a place of brilliance and purpose.

Surpassing the "10,000 hour" point of maximizing the talent of leaders and teams, her purpose is simple: help leaders and companies achieve their unique goals through healthy leadership and high-performance teams.

Known for her heart centered straight-talk and candor, Cyndi consults with CEOs and executives of lean, growing, organizations who are impatient for results. She's led hundreds of leaders through Coaching, and thousands through her self-created Leadership Development Training. In addition, more than 7,000 hiring decisions and career moves have been made thanks to Cyndi's expertise and guidance. She wants people to succeed in healthy cultures while also feeling the impact of success over the long haul.

With a degree in Marketing and Sales from The Culverhouse College of Business at The University of Alabama (Roll Tide), she has led numerous Procter & Gamble initiatives over her 10-year contribution with a focus in sales management/hiring/training, new venture startup, technology development, and strategic planning. After following her passion to elevate others, Cyndi also helped build a non-profit organization from a start-up with three employees to a $15 million+ enterprise with more than 100 employees and 2,400 volunteers from 1995 to 2005. Now having served as a consultant for 15+ years, Cyndi helps people stretch to their vision and goals.

Cyndi is always exploring new ideas to innovate and help others live with excitement and resilience; she credits her success to two furry and loyal followers, Happy and Camper, her English Retrievers.

Certifications:

- Holds the Advanced Senior Certified Birkman Consultant Certification, a distinction held by less than 5% of consultants certified with Birkman
- Holds a Professional Master Coaching Certification, a distinction held by 2% of coaches.
- Certified Life Coach
- Certified Life Plan Facilitator, and Alcohol Addiction Recovery Coach through LPCCI and IACET who are International Coach Federation certified
- Certified Professional Neuro-Linguistic Practitioner
- Life-time Associate of the Career Thought Leader Consortium
- Member of the Professional Association for Resume Writers

and Career Coaches

CONNECT WITH CYNDI WINEINGER:

https://www.linkedin.com/in/cyndi-wineinger/
http://www.thewineingercompany.com/
http://www.stretch-sl.com/

II.

A Legacy Worth Remembering

Where Culture & Leadership Collide

Melanie Booher, CEO & Entrepreneur

Be a leader worth following.

Seems pretty simple, right? Ahh, if only that were the case. We are pulled in a multitude of directions with all the notions of what compromises a successful leader. For example: motivate and engage your team, but don't be a cheerleader. Coach others and give direction, but don't micromanage. Ask good questions, but don't be too nosey. Bring your unique ideas and solutions to the table, but don't move forward until you have a group consensus. Ask your leader to help with big issues, but solve all the little issues yourself (oh – and by the way, all the issues are little issues!) Delegate things to others, but also be willing to get your hands dirty. Be strategic, but remember that sometimes you must get in the weeds and utilize your tactical skills. Praise in public, but be sure to always criticize in private. And the list goes on and on...

There is one staple in all of this advice that always holds true:

lead with respect (No one ever says, "Hey – it's okay to be a jerk!"). It's never okay! Respectful interactions are the foundation of great workplace culture. While everyone is ultimately held to this standard, the buck stops at what the Leadership Team is willing to tolerate and how they are behaving; especially when no one is looking. Strong leaders talk the talk and walk the walk – knowing that others are listening, watching, and emulating.

A leadership book isn't complete without some perspective on workplace culture – and how leaders are responsible for the tone within an organization. My first book, *Conscious Culture*, provides a detailed game plan for creating that great culture. Our template called the THRIVE™ Model helps you level-up your culture game, at work and home, by helping today's leaders succeed in tomorrow's world. Unlike other books about workplace culture, it builds on a heart-rooted foundation and utilizes a model in order to grow. We believe in maximizing people – more than just making money – and then everyone wins. We believe that together, we THRIVE™.

For this book, *Leadership Fusion*, I am building on the concepts within the THRIVE™ Model and suggesting some additional actions that leaders can take to create an amazing culture. These additional actions can and will foster how you are seen by others and ultimately frames your legacy.

To ensure we have takeaways (that's how we make sure action is being taken and good things are happening), I will suggest areas called **"Bring-it-to-Life" moments**. These indicate important ideas for action in creating your ideal workplace culture. After all, reading a really good book (or chapter) is one thing, but taking heed and implementing those great ideas is another. Don't allow these ideas to grow dusty – make them happen! In

3-6 months, your team will thank you for it! When you look back at your career and work life, you will be proud of the legacy you have built.

"It is not our job to toughen our children up to face a cruel and heartless world. It is our job to raise children who will make the world a little less cruel and heartless."

– L.R. Knost

I started my business as an entrepreneur and mom of three. I was tired of bad bosses, corporate America, and too many hours spent away from loved ones. If I was going to spend endless hours dedicated to my work and away from my family – well dang it, I wanted to enjoy that work time! I was certain that other parents and employees had to feel the same heart pangs when pulled to work. This desire fueled me, more than just for myself – I wanted to impact others' lives for the better, also.

When my daughter Madilynn brought home the book, *Pay It Forward* by Catherine Ryan Hyde, the wording immediately caught my attention.[1] At first, Madi and I started taking turns reading, as I knew my daughter struggled with reading and this would help her. However, what started as a homework chore turned into genuine bonding time – and something that we both looked forward to each evening. Others in the family took interest and slowly but surely the number of readers, listeners, and cuddlers increased. Eventually, it included the whole family. We looked forward to reading the book together every night. All five of us – huddled together, passing the book between us, and taking turns reading. Great family moments, without sibling bickering, that I remember fondly.

Of course, I love the premise of the book: Trevor takes his extra-credit school assignment – (THINK OF AN IDEA FOR WORLD CHANGE AND PUT IT INTO ACTION) and turns it into a vast movement of kindness and goodwill that spreads around the world.

The idea was simple: Do a *profound* good deed for three people and ask them each to "pay it forward" to three others who need help. And so, the exponential goodness spreads. Pay It Forward has become a movement that has changed lives around the world. Sometimes, we water it down by purchasing a coffee for the person behind us in line...but the thought is what matters here. It doesn't matter how small the gesture is. We just need to level up our *Pay It Forward* game!

It's with that same child-like enthusiasm and passion as Trevor in the novel that I often talk about the THRIVE Model™. It's a big dream and an even bigger goal – but it's what I truly hope could happen. Imagine the momentum of a few strong leaders, building their culture, engaging their team, and creating a few great places to work. All of those employees will surely be positively impacted. They have families and loved ones who they go home to at night, where they are happier, more engaged, and more connected. The snowball effect amplifies, and the positivity is contagious. And so it grows. It all starts with how we embrace the day ahead of us and the choice we make to improve ourselves and our work culture.

BRING IT TO LIFE MOMENT: Reflect on these questions:

- Is personal improvement a byproduct of the professional work that you are doing?
- Does your work make you a better person? Does it help others in some way?
- Is your workplace better because you are in it?
- Is your home life better because of the work you do outside of the home?
- How do you want to be remembered? What kind of legacy do you want to leave behind?

Good people create our great workplace cultures. If you have a wonderful workplace and make the mistake of hiring someone who is not a good person, you will know it. Your people will know it. Your culture will feel it. Can that person change and assimilate? Maybe, but not likely.

People are products of our history and past behaviors. Here's an example: if a person doesn't have the ethical standards that you desire within your team, it will be difficult to teach them those desired ethics and how to stand by them at all costs. Reprogramming years of what they deemed acceptable behavior is harder than hiring someone who is already aligned with those standards and demonstrates acceptable behaviors. Read that again: it's much easier to set the expectation for what good ethics means within your workplace culture and hire people who naturally fit that mold.

BRING IT TO LIFE MOMENT: Update Hiring Practices

We can impact our team the most by hiring the right people. Update your hiring practices and interview guides to ask the right questions; ones that build off the desired behaviors. Then, you can truly hire people who are a culture fit!

"Empathy is about standing in someone else's shoes, feeling with his/her heart,

seeing with his/her eyes. Not only is empathy hard to outsource or automate,

but it makes the world a better place."

– Daniel Pink

Everyone is not prepared to lead with heart – yet I believe everyone could do it with a shift in mindset and a plan for action. The first step: shift your mindset to one that truly believes we all deserve to enjoy our work and work environment. Then, start to build a plan and develop specific actions which will lead towards this improvement. Again, get the ball rolling. Each person or teammate that embraces this idea will help it grow exponentially.

The purpose of this chapter is quite simple: to help leaders understand the importance of their most important asset – their people. Rally their people around aligned values and habits. We must be more intentionally focused on culture, outline a plan to improve, and utilize resources, ideas, and strategic interventions to design an intentional culture strategy for our organizations.

It wasn't until I started working on corporate culture that I really thought about my personal values and those which I would want my family to bring to the table day in and day out. I wanted to come up with something that my children could remember. Therefore, I went through an exercise where I brainstormed with my husband. Then I created something that was memorable and easily repeatable so that my kids could keep it at the top of their minds. So, now in the rush of mornings as we scurry out the door, quick kiss goodbye, and head off to school, we often repeat these poignant words:

"Be sweet. Be smart. Be strong. Be of service. "

– Melanie Booher

These words carry a lot of meaning for our family, more than just face value. We talk to the kids about what these words mean and how these are the values that our family is built upon. These words have turned into our family values. What are the behaviors and habits that support these keys to success? How do we want our family name to be represented? It's a matter of family pride and often a strong discussion point. Like the time that my son wanted to tell me how strong he was because he was going to fight all the boys at the playground. (Insert eye roll here) Okay, son, that's not exactly what mommy meant by strong. We mean "mentally strong" or "strong enough to stick up for others who are not able to." As you can imagine, that was an important discussion and moment for my son. His understanding of "strength" was redefined.

BRING IT TO LIFE MOMENT: Apply Culture Personally

I would encourage everyone to go through a personal exercise like what is described above and develop values and common language that resonates with their family. It ensures that we have important discussions with our kids about their character and how we treat others and what it means to represent your family with pride ("That's just how the Booher family is!"); but it will also make your heart happy.

"Talented people will come for the culture/mission, but they will leave due to poor managers/leaders. "

– Melanie Booher

You have likely heard this phrase before: "People don't leave companies, they leave bad managers." I cannot stress this enough: organizations today need more than merely involved leaders; they need inspiring ones. Leaders who engage others and are worth following. Leaders who are worth getting up every day and leaving your family and loved ones for long hours, because they are worthy of your time and talent.

Does your organization have what it takes to engage and retain your talent? Exit interview data will speak volumes, so be sure to assess those trends. Creating and ensuring leadership is bought in is one of the biggest obstacles to strengthening a company's culture. We simply must have leaders who lead by example or get out of the way – better yet – we move them out of the way. We control our own cultural destiny and I guarantee it's better not left up to chance.

"I AM the straw that stirs the drink"

– David Rains

Culture enhancement needs a nudge in the right direction and a little extra support. Typically, this is because leaders can have the best of intentions, but their plate is extremely full. And the thought of adding another thing to that plate...well, that just doesn't sit well.

Here's the thing: culture cannot be another flash in the pan, or chasing of the bright shiny object, only to be forgotten the next time a novel idea comes around. Culture may not strike "urgent" on the meter of things to focus on, but it will always be important and should always be a priority. Strong leaders plan ahead and take time to focus on important matters (even when they don't seem pressing). Be one of those leaders. Create your plan. Work your plan. When you do you will be in the elite 10% of those who are intentional in driving culture.

BRING IT TO LIFE MOMENT – Create strong culture habits.

The way to ensure culture doesn't get placed on the bookshelf to grow dusty within your organization is to instill THRIVE Model™ elements into your habits. There is power in understanding a habit. Once a habit becomes solidly rooted in your life, it becomes automatic. Once a habit gets rooted in your work, it becomes a ritual. The THRIVE™ Model urges leaders to focus on the roots first, then build and strengthen that foundation. Continue to build upward, shine a light on those areas that need attention, prune others that don't fit; and create the ongoing growth that you want to see in the branches.

James Clear has a book called *Atomic Habits: An Easy & Proven Way to Build Good Habits & Break Bad Ones*, which I encourage everyone to read.[2] One of my favorite tactics that I learned from James is the concept of "habit stacking."

To do this, simply identify a habit that you already do each day (like brushing your teeth) and add a habit that you want to develop to it or "stack" this new behavior on top of it. I used this approach to help me find time to write each day. When I get my coffee, I then sit down and write for a bit. Even if it is only fifteen minutes. Thus, a new habit is developed (and, in my case, a book is written! Yay!).

The need for a strong culture isn't going away any time soon. If anything, times of turmoil and change accentuate the need for strong culture as employers struggle to navigate the changes tossed their way. People today are facing more adversity than ever – from additional stress at home, to social upheaval, political turmoil, global illness, and wars – and those are just the things we know about. Strong leaders recognize that we simply cannot keep piling it on and hope that employees can maintain the same level of productivity and morale.

Yet, with all this happening in the world, humans still maintain a somewhat simple desire: to enjoy whatever path we choose for ourselves. For most, it's a path that spans the majority of our daytime hours (ahh...the joy of work!) Therefore, the importance of workplace culture is paramount. Good people deserve a good work environment. Leaders simply cannot ignore the significance of workplace culture.

It's critical that leaders do what's best for their people. So, many organizations assign the task of culture to someone on the team in an effort to implement some of these ideas/projects internally in order to save money. What we have found most often, is that leadership teams are "trusting their gut" and assume that because they are "good with people" they can create a good workplace culture.

Few people actually have a tangible plan, and planning is an essential element. My goal here is to provide some ideas for leaders to drive culture forward in an intentional way but without breaking the bank. Here's some good news: we have a few options that are at a variety of price ranges. Here are a few ways that leaders drive strong culture within organizations:

BRING IT TO LIFE MOMENT: Utilize the THRIVE™ Model

Obviously, this is my favorite tool. (Warning: there could be some bias here given that I created it!) However, my team also believes in this tool wholeheartedly. In fact, we believe in it so much that we give it away for FREE. We use it to support companies as they make sense of their culture and organize all the elements needed in order to build a strong foundation and grow from there. From roots to branches, we are reviewing processes and practices that make our culture stronger. People Operations/Human Resources support this journey, as they are the main proponents of the processes addressed within the model.

Putting a physical (written) plan in place is the key. Join less than 10% of companies that actually plan for their culture. The THRIVE Model™ helps leaders do more than just trust their gut. Create a plan, garner alignment so that everyone is on the same page, make continual improvements, and apply the power of habit. You will see the results in morale, productivity, turnover, and more. The good news: it will generate a competitive advantage and ensure a resilient legacy. Bonus: did I mention that this tool is FREE? Details are outlined in my book Conscious Culture and you can print a copy from our website.

BRING IT TO LIFE MOMENT: Get a Mentor/Coach

I'm a firm believer that everyone needs a coach or mentor and should also be a coach/mentor to someone else. Often, as leaders progress up the ladder of success, we stop utilizing professional development (training, coaches, etc.) because we believe that our own knowledge and experience outweigh the contributions of a coach.

There is a fallacy of thinking here. Leaders must be willing to listen and learn new things, as we all have blind spots and areas which need growth. Personal/professional development is more like a jungle gym: we progress forwards, sideways, and sometimes backward, to get the right footing and eventually move upwards and onwards.

Personal and business coaches, or consultants, are booming in a big way as we all work towards ongoing success for this year and beyond. The world of being a Culture Coach is a relatively new one, but it's much needed. I have a variety of clients who happily sign up for Culture Therapy (or a Culture Strategy Session) in order to keep their Culture & People plan moving forward, brainstorm new ideas, and hold themselves accountable.

Whether you need help with sales, navigating LinkedIn, general success, organization, mindfulness, wellness, conscious business leadership...the list goes on and on – there's bound to be a coach for you. Ask for referrals to coaches, interview coaches of interest, and ultimately find the best one that fits your needs. Through partnerships, networking groups, and the company Influence Network Media – all kinds of coaches/consultants come to mind. Making good introductions and being a people connector is a passion of mine, so connect with me! I'm happy to support you on your coach/mentor journey. BONUS: some of my favorites are writing with me in *Leadership Fusion*...so keep reading!

Similarly, it's important to find others to mentor/coach as well. I have been participating in a student mentoring program for HR students at the University of Cincinnati for the last couple of years. Tom Mobley has done an amazing job with that program and I'm happy to support him and his students. I've been lucky to meet some wonderful kids – many of whom I keep in touch with – and I have pulled a few into HR project work when possible. In fact, one of my early students became my first intern with MB Consulting. We met at the SHRM National Meeting in Washington, DC a few years back and have been friends and colleagues ever since. The joy of watching your student grow up in their HR role, change jobs, and/or get promoted is incredibly rewarding. What's really cool about this reward is that it goes both ways!

BRING IT TO LIFE MOMENT: Play Cards for Culture©

A new idea for alignment and progress is a game called Cards for Culture©: The Business Edition. Some have compared the game to Apples to Apples or Cards Against Humanity but with a culture approach – but we don't want to set the bar too high!

While there are some similarities, our game drives a good discussion to help clarify what your culture means and how to embed it through habits within your workplace. This revolutionary game literally places company culture in your own hands through three different decks of cards.

Even if you already have Vision & Values noted within your organization, most employees can't reiterate them. Memorization is not happening. Sadly, confusion abounds. With all of that in mind, we have created a unique and fun way for leadership teams to build camaraderie, improve communication, foster trust, and align expectations related to organizational culture.

Gamification of culture is new and exciting; it's a critical step in building engagement among your leadership team. So, gather your top leaders (obtain a facilitator if desired to help with time management, defusing situations, and holding players accountable), and set aside some time to determine your Keys for Success, Defining Behaviors, and Habits.

Gamifying culture with Cards for Culture© makes it memorable, and fun, and yields quick results. Our client, Peter Schulteis, gave the game a rave review by stating, "We got more done in two hours than we have in ten years!" Here are the bonuses: amazing discussions, team building, communication clarity, and behavior alignment will follow.

BRING IT TO LIFE MOMENT: Use Assessments with your Team

There are a few types of assessments on the market and I recommend using one to help gather information on employee behavioral styles.

DISC: One of my favorite tools is the DISC assessment and Mark Allen is my go-to guy for getting these done. Google refers to DISC as the "best-selling, non-judgmental personality and behavioral assessment used by more than one million people every year to improve teamwork, communication, and productivity."

What I really like about DISC, is the fact that many people are aware of it, have taken a DISC assessment, and have an idea of what their personality style is. The kicker and multiplier for DISC is to really take the time to understand how you can adjust your style to better work with others and help you understand them better as well. Taking the assessment but letting the information grow old isn't a good recipe. Flex that DISC muscle and keep talking about those DISC profiles and how you relate to others.

E3/Management Essentials: Our behaviors dictate the results we achieve in the boardroom and the dining room. Understanding how we behave is the first step toward improving our results. The E3 Behavioral Assessment is an effective, simple, scientifically validated, cloud-based tool that measures key behaviors and motivators. It consists of selecting adjectives that represent your preferences and only take five-eight minutes to complete. E3 scores you in everything from Aggression to Support, Criticality to Creativity. Results for key performers create benchmarks to evaluate candidates. Those for teams or organizations define the behaviors representative of an organization's culture. At its core, culture is the way things are done (e.g. behaviors). A big thank you to John Lucas for introducing me to the E3!

Wrapping Up

Culture and leadership go hand in hand. This is not rocket science, but they both involve investing in people – because good people are the heart of great organizations. Those good people need a plan and support (the abundance of ideas mentioned here, structured by The THRIVE Model™). Believe in your team, but also take action. Give them tools to level up and construct habits to make living the values of the organization second nature. Then, leaders can build the culture of dreams; and if you build it, they will stay.

Throughout the US, we are in the midst of a human movement. Life-changing challenges around the world have surfaced feelings of isolation and indifference, fear, and sadness. For some, work is the escape they need from personal chaos at home. For others, work is just something they do to pass the time until they get to be with loved ones again.

If leaders want to see organizational success in their respective markets, it's absolutely essential to ensure the organization's culture is part of the competitive advantage and that it shines. We can do this by being intentional and utilizing the THRIVE Model's™ 6 key areas and new ideas for action to help guide that intentional strategy. Being purposeful in the culture we desire to create.

Remember, as David Rains said, "Rome wasn't built in a day."

We cannot do everything at once. Gradual improvement and culture-building take time and continual focus. It takes commitment to the cause, creating a plan, and working on that plan. We cannot simply hope for the best and trust our gut. We know too much about the importance of a strong culture to be that naïve. And when we know better, we can – and should – do better.

Hopefully, you now have a better understanding of the important link between culture and leadership. Explained in many ways, the fundamental idea is that there's a deeper connection between strong leaders and the strong cultures that we so desire in our workplace.

Like Trevor said in the book, *Pay it Forward*, we must take the assignment seriously:

"THINK OF AN IDEA FOR WORLD CHANGE AND PUT IT INTO ACTION"

Are you ready to create a movement that will change lives for the better? Here in our immediate personal surroundings, in organizations, within our state, country, and around the world? The power lies in the momentum of a few strong leaders, building culture, leading with respect, and creating great places to work. Imagine all of the employees who can be positively impacted. And their families/loved ones who they go home to at night, experiencing this strong leadership/great culture movement as a positive offshoot in their home lives, as well. They are happier, more engaged, and more connected.

Positivity is contagious. It starts with making the choice to be better. Embrace the day ahead of you. Make the right choice, time and time again. Lead with heart. Ask yourself: what do we want to be known for? What kind of legacy do we want to leave behind? We answer these questions and make the conscious decision to be a good person and strong leader, and have the beginning of an amazing culture legacy.

This concept is the first step; sharing it and encouraging leaders to take steps forward. Baby steps if needed – just keep moving forward. We can grow beyond our roots, beyond the leaves...the sky is the limit. You will see exponential growth and enhanced leadership skills. Culture is the multiplier.

Given your choice in leisure time and obvious good taste in books (this one!) – it's clear that you are already part of this culture-shaping movement. Culture is a collective commitment that is bigger than any one of us. As leaders, we can "pay it forward so that everyone gets the culture that they deserve. We can leave the world a better place than we found it. One good person, one strong leader, one game plan, and one great work culture at a time.

And so, leaders, take action. Spend time working on yourself and your leadership skills, engage your team, and utilize the BRING IT TO LIFE MOMENTS. These indicate important ideas for action – an action that strong leaders take to create a great workplace culture.

It's up to you. Failure is not an option. Success is within your reach. The plan is right here – implement it! Then, when you proudly reminisce about the journey to becoming a great leader, building a strong culture, leading with heart, to creating and implementing a culture plan, the end result will support the hard work that you have put in. You can be proud of the legacy you built. A legacy worth remembering. Bring it to life – now is your moment.

Notes

1. Hyde, Catherine Ryan. Pay It Forward. Simon & Schuster Books for Young Readers, 2014.
2. Clear, James. Atomic Habits: An Easy &Proven Way to Build Good Habits & Break Bad Ones. Avery, 2018.

Melanie Booher

Melanie Booher is a veteran business leader who strives to make the world better – one workplace at a time. With more than twenty years of business experience, Melanie develops leaders across three dimensions: through individual development, by inspiring and guiding leaders to find and share their voice, through team development, by harnessing the power of habit to influence people, and through organizational improvement, by spurring change to create workplace cultures that THRIVE.

Melanie is the President of Influence Network Media and PEOPLEfirst Talent & Retention Consulting. She's the creator of the THRIVE™ Model, Cards for Culture©, and the Conscious Culture Certified Coach program.

Melanie believes that great cultures represent a collective commitment that is bigger than any one of us. She inspires others to create a pay-it-forward legacy – leaving the world a better place than we found it. One good person, one game plan, one great work culture at a time. Join the movement – impacting retention, productivity, and profit – but most importantly knowing that together we THRIVE^{TM}!

Her books Conscious Culture and Talent Fusion launched in 2021, with a few more underway! Melanie enjoys travel, golf, photography, kids' sports and long walks on the beach. She lives outside of Cincinnati, OH with her husband and three children.

Melanie holds a Bachelor's Degree from Miami University and a Master's Degree in HR from the University of Cincinnati. She has worked for powerhouses like Macy's, Cintas, Provident & National City Bank, and Charming Shoppes. She is a certified Culture Coach with CultureWise (2019) and Conscious Culture (2021). Her book and game are leading the market in gamification of culture – check them out!

Melanie has a proven track record as a Culture Coach helping organizations become a "Best Place to Work" by instilling big-company best practices within an entrepreneurial environment. Rooted in her experiences as a people connector, change agent, and business coach – she drives organizations to truly live their values, not just post them on the conference room walls.

CONNECT WITH MELANIE BOOHER:

You should contact Melanie when you need help with:

- Culture Strengthening
- Leadership Development
- Fractional HR & Recruitment
- Diversity Equity & Inclusion Programs
- Leveling-up your People Operations/HR

LinkedIn: https://www.linkedin.com/in/melanie-booher/

Connect via email: melanie@thrivewithmb.com
http://www.thrivewithmb.com/
http://calendly.com/thrivewithmb

12.

The Role of the CRO

Why Sales Leadership is Needed in the C-Suite

Angela Rakis, President and Founder of Metis Sales Solutions

It's been a long time coming, but finally, the sales organization is represented in the C-Suite of companies. Although there are a few different variations of the title, the Chief Revenue Officer accurately articulates the job and responsibility of this senior executive. Their job is larger than simply securing new clients for the company. Their larger role is to bring the entire organization into the process of improving the customer experience and building teamwork.

Driving revenue into a company in a repeatable and sustainable fashion requires the support of all senior leaders and therefore having a CRO in your C-Suite has become an obvious need. Sales is not a solitary transaction, nor is it an independent organization. The sales team requires the support of all divisions of the company to truly make significant progress and revenue growth. Revenue growth increases exponentially when the entire organization is encouraged to support this crucial element and included in the celebration of the company's overall success.

As a sales leader who has worked at extremely large global organizations, as well as having supported small local businesses, I have seen the positive effect of having support for the sales team from the CEO down through the entire team. There have also been negative effects when divisions of an organization refused to support the sales team. Salespeople have long been the outcasts in an organization, receiving criticism and scrutiny from other teams. The people at the office who are delivering services only see that the sales team is frequently out of the office traveling to different locations, dining out with clients, and turning in large expense reports. However, when others within the office are asked if they want to be in on the sales team, the answer is a quick "No, thank you." The other teams will distance themselves from the sales team because of their lack of willingness to understand how the sales team does their job. This situation, if tolerated by the senior leadership team, greatly inhibits the success of the salesperson. I have personally watched two divisions in a company achieve dramatically different results simply because one salesperson was supported completely in their division and another salesperson was not supported by the team.

A CEO and CRO have the responsibility to educate the extended teams on the value of working with the sales team to provide excellent customer service and accelerate revenue growth. The CEO that creates an environment focused on enabling and supporting the sales team brings everyone together for a common goal of growing the company.

Changing The Sales Approach

A long time ago there was a sales team philosophy: don't confuse selling with implementation. The goal was to just go sell. It didn't matter how the scope of work was going to get done. That outdated strategy needs to be replaced with a new, upgraded one. The sales team must understand the effect they have on the rest of the organization if there is truly going to be a culture where the sales team is supported throughout.

Historically, a salesperson could sell what appeared to be an amazing deal for the company only to find out that the operations team could not deliver on the promises the salesperson had committed to. This often results in the operations team being extremely frustrated and mad at the salesperson for setting them up for failure and therefore not wanting to work with the salesperson again. It also creates resentment with customer service because the unhappy and dissatisfied client will constantly call the office angry, yelling and taking it out on customer service. Therefore, the customer service team resents the sales team. Important details in the client contracts would cause complications because the sales team didn't understand the nuances of terms and clauses in the contract. Finally, not knowing all of the numbers and finances around an opportunity can create deals that look great in the beginning, but are essentially turned upside down and lose the company money because things aren't taken into consideration.

These types of situations create animosity and frustration, all focused on the salesperson. This is the exact situation that gets resolved by having the CRO in the C-Suite and the entire company working together with sales rather than against. The idea of the entire company working together and supporting sales is two-fold. One aspect is that they communicate and the salesperson understands the effect their deals have on the rest of the organization and conversely. The entire company working together also shows the rest of the organization the effect they have in delivering a quality solution that generates more revenue for the company.

Sales isn't a solitary transaction or an independent event that is owned by a single salesperson. True sales success starts long before the salesperson is engaged. It starts at the top with leadership. The culture that is established for the company and expectations from the team set the tone for teamwork and success. Enabling sales leadership to engage in all organizations throughout the company allows them to partner with the other teams for joint success.

CEO – Company Culture

As the CEO of a company, it's obvious that the end goal is to build the company, meaning growth of revenue for the business owners and stakeholders. It's not to say that this is the only goal and mission, but it is the obvious measurement that is tracked. As the CEO creates their corporate culture, many things are considered and one of those needs to be how are they going to support the sales activities. Consider where revenue needs to come from: look at new clients that need to be obtained as well as the retention of existing clients and subsequently, the growth of revenue from each individual client. The sales team is often focused on net new client acquisition. However, the rest of the organization needs to be assisted in the retention and growth of extension existing clients.

Helping the team recognize the important role that they play in the success of the company and how their role fits into the life cycle and lifetime value of the client is crucial. The entire company needs to feel as though they are one team working together for that unified goal.

Marketing – One Voice

Sales and marketing have always had a love/hate relationship of sorts. The fact is that the personality type that makes a good marketer is often the opposite of the personality type that makes a good salesperson. Although the two groups are constantly frustrated with each other, they do recognize the need that they have for each other and understand how when they come together as a single team, the success is exponential. Marketing is needed to build brand awareness to engage prospective clients and help the company find its voice. Too many times, young companies are too focused on sales and want to grow sales and their client acquisition without first investing in marketing.

This strategy simply won't work in the longrun. As a salesperson, if you call on a prospective client and that client searches for your company on the Internet to find a terrible webpage, no presence on any social media, and a lack of reviews or customer testimonials, the conversation with the salesperson will end quickly. As a company, you need a reputation and it's the entire organization's responsibility to build that positive reputation; however, it's the marketing team's responsibility to get that reputation out into the world. It's simply not enough to be amazing at what you do and has happy clients, you must also build your reputation and presence within the community and business world.

Once the marketing strategy is formed, that messaging needs to be communicated throughout the organization. Everyone in the company should be able to articulate the services and products offered and their value proposition. One of the first things I do when I engage with new clients is to ask various members of the organization what they do/sell. I am always surprised at the variety of answers I receive. Even in the sales team, the explanations can vary if the marketing messaging isn't appropriately communicated to the team. Your clients and prospective clients need to be hearing the same, consistent messaging from everyone in the company. As the CEO and leadership team, it is your responsibility to communicate your vision to the marketing team and subsequently, to the rest of the organization.

Sales – Go Get 'Em

Investing in the sales team is crucial to the success of that sales team. Although you are likely hiring quality and experienced salespeople, they still need to come together as a team with a cohesive strategy and process. Creating a sales playbook ensures that team members are all following the same process and rules. They should all understand the sales messaging from marketing, who they should be targeting, and the value proposition to be articulating to prospects.

It may not seem like you need to do sales training, but bringing the team together to talk through their experiences, as well as wins and loses, will increase the win-rate for the entire team. Hearing each sales member clearly articulating the solution and value proposition allows for you to be sure everyone is representing your company appropriately. Similarly, sales training should be offered to the client-services team as well. They will be an important part of identifying add-on opportunities with existing clients.

Finally, implementing a Client Relationship Management (CRM) software solution to track opportunity progress, agent activity, and accurate forecasting helps the entire organization keep up-to-date with potential new business. Holding regular communications with the extended team on the sales activities helps those extended teams to be prepared in assisting the sales activity; as well as a ramp for new business.

CFO – Know your numbers

The CFO and the finance team have a significant impact on how prices should be set and what negotiation opportunities the salespeople can participate in. Having the finance team work directly with the sales team helps the sales team understand clearly what the overall goals are. This collaboration also allows sales to negotiate quicker and more successfully with prospects.

If the business goal of the company is revenue-focused, then the negotiations the salesperson has with the prospect are different than if the company is more profit-focused. Salespeople also have the ability to affect cash flow through their salesmanship and contract opportunities. If the salesperson is enabled with these types of details and understands the threshold for each, then they can negotiate directly with the client and avoid slowing down the sell cycle by asking the client permission during every conversation.

A well-written compensation plan for the salesperson will drive the behavior you need from your clients in order to achieve those revenue goals. Creating a pricing worksheet that allows the salesperson to know exactly where the profit margin is per opportunity allows them to price and negotiate their deals and adjust the price accordingly

Legal – Non-Negotiables

Similarly, the legal team's involvement in educating and working with the sales team is critical. There are certain situations and structures to a contract that are simply non-negotiable for a company. Alternatively, there are items that are open to discussion and revision. The salesperson needs to know what both of those are prior to entering into contractual conversations with the prospect. By letting the salesperson know upfront what these items of negation and non-negotiables are, the sales team can drive the best contract for the company and close the deal more quickly.

Items that are easily negotiable but can drive revenue to the company are contract length, termination clause, and payment terms elements. These items can help support the company and provide give and take between the salesperson and the prospect during negotiation. Providing the sales team with the standard client contract containing highlighted areas of negotiation they are authorized to negotiate for the company, allows them to drive more revenue for the company, be more creative, and close deals faster.

Operations – We Need Some Help Over Here

Often, the operations team is called in to support a sales effort. As the sales team explains the product services and offerings of your company, clients will want some reassurance that the promises that the salesperson makes can be delivered by the operations team. This goes back to the point of not confusing sales with implementation and the terrible reputation that can be created for a salesperson. There are also situations where the services being delivered are extremely complex and a technical person is needed to have those more detailed, in-depth conversations with the prospect. How you align your operations team with the sales team will depend on the services and products you offer. It may simply be that some leadership or management role from operations needs to attend this single meeting or a lunch with the prospective client just to make sure the handoff between one organization to another goes smoothly. In a more complex environment, true sales engineers are needed, and service delivery managers may also be needed to get engaged to help facilitate the handoff and the implementation of the new scope of work. If the person from operations that is supporting sales is a role that generates revenue, meaning you bill their hours out to other clients (or they are assigned to another client), then you need to be careful not to overburden them with sales responsibilities as they do not want to disappoint current clients. If that's the situation, you'll need to consider ways to compensate and encourage those people to step away from their main roles and responsibilities to support the sales team.

If your organization is large enough that you have dedicated team members in operations that support the sales team, be sure to watch that they do not become too distant and isolated from day-to-day operations. Be sure that they know the reality of what your operations team can deliver. Too often, the sales support teams get involved in sales activities and when operational changes occur within your company they are not informed and don't know that service delivery has been edited. The salesperson and their support teammate can end up misrepresenting capabilities to the prospective client.

Customer Service – Retain and Expand

Customer service plays such a crucial role in retaining and expanding services provided to existing clients. Often, when I provide sales training to customer service teams, I am met with a tremendous amount of resistance. Their view of salespeople, like most, is that salespeople are pushy and unpopular and many have no desire to play this role. However, when the sales training is complete, the customer service team comes to realize that sales is solving problems for clients, which is exactly what client services do every single day. The role in client services is to field those questions and complaints from a current client and solve them. This job is crucial to the revenue of the company in retaining existing clients. Additionally, it's significantly easier to sell more services to an existing client than it is to acquire a new client. The customer service team is in a prime position to do just that for your organization. Larger organizations may hire a sales team specifically to work with existing clients focused on expanding the services that are provided to them, but in a smaller organization customer service has that responsibility.

It's not an easy transition to make to get the customer service team comfortable with their sales role; however, once you do, revenue can quickly grow within your customer base. After taking client services through sales training, the customer service teams often have more respect for the salespeople and are more willing to engage a salesperson when they have a question or a growth opportunity. Helping customer service understands the language and the goals of the sales team and the process of selling improves their confidence as well as the sales team's satisfaction in partnering with them on opportunities. Once you have the entire team speaking the same language, using the same processes, asking good questions, and uncovering new opportunities together, team satisfaction improves greatly.

Accounting – Absolutely part of the team

The accounting department is absolutely part of the revenue-generating team. They don't just collect the money after all the hard work has been done and they should not be the bad guy in the end if things go wrong. Having a good relationship between the sales team and the accounting department will help with the retention of existing clients and cash flow into the company.

When a new client is secured, a clear handoff to the accounting department is also a valuable step to add to the process. Help the accounting department know who to invoice, how the client would like to be invoiced, confirm terms and conditions that were negotiated, and any other nuances and requests from the client to speed up the onboarding process and therefore revenue into the company. It's the salesperson's responsibility to either gather this information for the accounting team or to make the introduction between your accounting department and the new client's accounting department so that they can work out the details between themselves. I have seen more than one deal lost because the accounting department was inflexible or unpleasant to work with. This does not have to happen if sales and accounting can work together so that expectations are set from the beginning with the new client and with the internal accounting department.

Once this partnership is established, the accounting team will feel empowered to reach out to the sales team when a client isn't paying and before they send anyone to collections or terminate a contract for non-payment. The salesperson is the one that made that agreement with the client and should be given an opportunity to go speak with that client and understand the problem or issue. We all know many things happen in day-to-day business and there is a multitude of reasons why a client may not pay; however, allowing the salesperson an opportunity to save the contract helps everybody.

Everybody Sells

Considering the number of teams within a company that the sales team needs to collaborate with when performing their job, and the significant impact they have on the success of the company, elevating the CRO to the C-Suite is a clear necessity. Sales leadership needs the authority to drive change into the entire organization to support the business goals and vision of the CEO.

Through working on hundreds of opportunities and consulting with customers of all sizes, I have come to realize the importance of the "everyone sells" philosophy. I've actually created a workshop for my clients to help take them through this process. We map out every single stage of the selling cycle and identify who is talking with the client and in what ways they can support the sell cycle. Everyone from the receptionist who answers the initial phone call and schedules a technician, to the salesperson who comes to visit, to the final step of collecting invoicing and billing, everyone is vital and plays a very important part in the overall success of the company. The success of the company is revenue focused and revenue is dependent on client satisfaction and delivering what is promised to the client.

As the CEO of the company, it is your job to encourage all divisions to support the sales department. Elevate sales leadership to a Chief Revenue Officer role and include them in your C-Suite. This will empower them to reach out and gain the support necessary to truly drive change in the company. The ability to grow revenue in a holistic fashion and build a team culture that respects and supports each other is truly the future of corporate growth. When you can see that every department in the organization is positively affected by the sales team, and everyone is celebrating their effort, you are on the fast track to success.

If you need help in achieving this vision, please do not hesitate to reach out to me. I consult with companies to develop their sales strategies, build a sales team and set up the tools and resources needed to drive revenue. After 25 years in sales, I have practical experience that I can share with you and your team.

Angela Rakis

Angela Rakis is the President and Founder of Metis Sales Solutions, a sales consulting firm. Angela leverages her 20+ years of selling and sales leadership to help business clients implement growth strategies to realize their revenue potential and increase confidence in their sales team and processes.

Prior to founding Metis Sales Solutions, Angela led sales teams at Fortune 500 organizations like IBM and Xerox, as well as mid-market firms across the country. Throughout her sales career, she has cultivated success by developing unique thought leadership and sales strategies while establishing loyal and profitable relationships with clients. Teams have relied on Angela for her ability to retain clients, turn around troubled relationships, and build confidence that they can close deals, manage clients, and be an industry leader.

CONECT WITH ANGELA RAKIS:

http://linkedin.com/in/angela-rakis-158188

MetisSalesSolutions.com

13.

Sales Enablement

The #1 Missing Element in Go-To-Market Strategy

Simcha Kackley, CEO and Founder of Swivel

*BONUS: Score YOUR Go-To-Market Strategy with a 7-Question Quiz

What Today's Buyers Need

Buying has changed over the last ten years. We live in a world of instant gratification. Buyers don't have to wait anymore – they can get their groceries delivered to them on the same day, they can get Amazon orders in 1-click, and they can find explicit comparisons of you vs. your competitors online in minutes. Googling is their initial reflex rather than picking up the phone to talk to someone. And they expect their experiences to be tailored to their needs every step of the way.

B2B Buying Trends

It's clear that your buyers are doing the majority of their B2B, or business-to-business, purchasing online before even reaching a salesperson. In fact, buyers are 70% of the way through their buying research before contacting sales.

The B2B Buyers' Journey

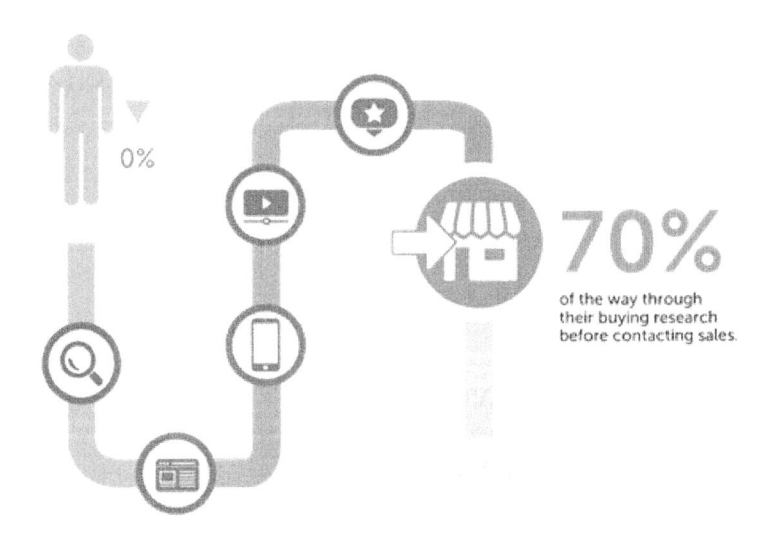

0%

70% of the way through their buying research before contacting sales.

Updating Your Sales Models

So, if all this has changed, that means your sales model needs to change, too. Sales teams stuck in traditional ways of doing business simply can't meet buyers' evolving needs. You can't rely on the same strategies, like controlling the buyer's access to information, and expect the same results.

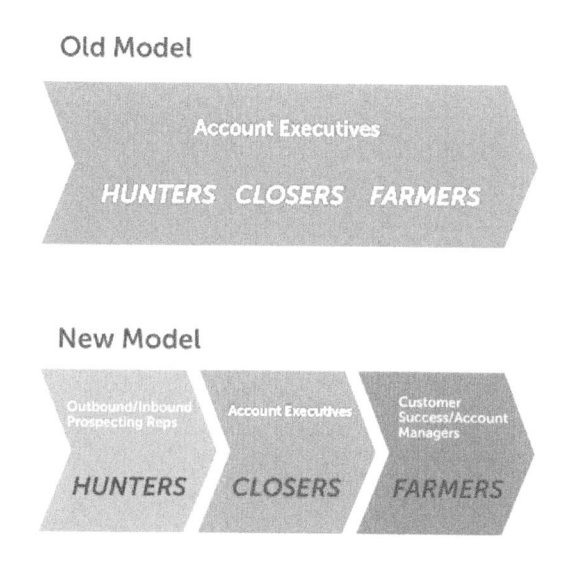

Old Model

Account Executives

HUNTERS CLOSERS FARMERS

New Model

Outbound/Inbound Prospecting Reps	Account Executives	Customer Success/Account Managers
HUNTERS	CLOSERS	FARMERS

In addition to changing buyer behavior, it's important to consider the structure of the sales team, too. Traditional models with salespeople managing the whole process just don't work. Salespeople are being asked to do much – hunt, close, and farm. These are very different roles that require different strengths, skills, and experience.

This old model doesn't set salespeople up for success—which can be frustrating to your sales team. According to the Bridge Group research, B2B sales turnover is 34%.[1] This high of rate is unsustainable and indicates there's a problem. Many of the people surveyed in this research said burnout was one of the key reasons for leaving a company. When you push your team for stronger results without giving them the tools they need to get those results, you end up pushing them out the door.

B2B sales turnover is 34%

The Problem

Most sales teams aren't set up to meet the needs of today's buyers—they're stuck in that old model. For these sales reps, their day-to-day work might look something like this:

- Cold calling people who don't have a need or buying intent
- Fully manual processes limiting how many prospects they can reach
- No content or resources to increase the velocity of the sale
- An inability to reach and connect with the best prospects because they don't have quality firmographic data on their ideal customers

These outdated strategies hinder the results your sales team can achieve. This imbalance between expectations and enablement means salespeople on these teams are **losing their mojo**.

Sales
people
are
losing
their
mojo.

The inefficiencies and outdated approaches aren't just frustrating for the reps. They lead to bigger issues for the company.

Declining Margins
Without strong differentiation, your profit margins decrease (and you become a commodity).

Declining Close Rates
Increasing competitive pressure causes you to lose more deals.

Declining Opportunities
Your sales people can't hunt as effectively as they used to, meaning less "at bats."

The Reflex

When a salesperson doesn't drive the revenue they're expected to in the time required, what does leadership do?

- Fire them and hire someone new
- Hire more sales reps on their team
- Invest in sales training
- Create a better website or sales deck
- Hire multiple agencies
- Hire an entry-level marketing manager who won't know what to do and needs a budget

Hiring new people won't help if the framework isn't optimized. Getting a better website or hiring an agency won't help if the model is broken.

Believe it or not:
Growth no longer relies on growing your sales force.

Smart organizations are strategically maximizing and empowering their salespeople to get ahead – through a modern approach to sales enablement. When this happens, companies shift from the old ways of doing sales, like cold calling and relationship-focused meetings, to more effective methods, like strategic lead generation, prioritization, and personalization.

Go from what we call "brute-force growth" to scalable growth.

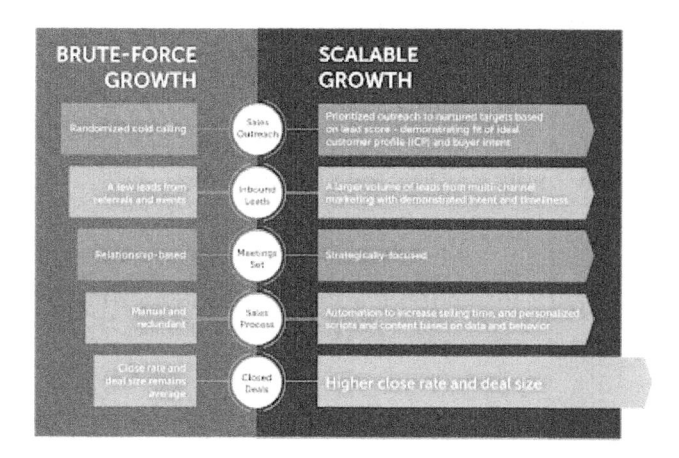

The #1 Missing Element in Your Go-To-Market Strategy is Sales Enablement

The biggest opportunity for growth lies in a system that aligns sales, marketing, and technology on a Go-To-Market strategy, with teams that work collaboratively to activate it together. At the root of this system is sales enablement.

Sales Enablement

What is Sales Enablement?

Most definitions of sales enablement just focus on the end result for the sales reps. Take this definition from SiriusDecisions, for example:

"The goal of sales enablement is to ensure reps possess the skills, knowledge, assets, and process expertise to maximize every buyer interaction."

Or, they only focus on training and content:

"Sales enablement is the strategic, ongoing process of equipping sales teams with the content, guidance, and training they need to effectively engage buyers" – Highspot[2]

These explanations are a great start, but they miss the bigger picture. Truly effective sales enablement needs to start before the rep gets the leads. It starts with the whole Go-To-Market strategy.

A better definition of sales enablement is:

"Development and execution of a Go-To-Market strategy in collaboration with marketing, sales, and leadership that prioritizes lead generation of, and sales efforts on, prospects with buying intent, as well as the resources sales teams need to maximize interactions with those buyers – to ultimately increase close rate, velocity, and deal size."

This definition works better because it focuses on the prioritization of all your marketing and sales efforts. If every buyer your sales team is reaching is not sales-ready, then we don't need to maximize that buyer interaction – we need to change which buyers the sales teams are reaching in the first place!

Prioritization: Start at the Bottom of the Funnel

The best way to prioritize your efforts is to start at the bottom of the funnel and work your way up. Starting at the bottom of the funnel is most strategic and results in the lowest customer acquisition cost and highest margin.

```
COLD AUDIENCE
THINKING ABOUT CATEGORY
HIGHLY TARGETED NAMED ACCOUNTS
READY TO BUY
EXISTING CUSTOMERS
```

Existing Customers

Cross-selling existing customers should come before acquiring new ones. These prospects already know and trust you, which results in a much lower acquisition cost. You can reach these customers in an outbound multi-touch campaign to maximize the relationship and brand equity.

Ready to Buy

The right message at the right TIME is everything. This audience is based on behavioral online triggers that demonstrate intent to buy your solutions. For example, someone is leaning in if they are conducting a google search for your products or competitors, or posting on their social media looking for recommendations.

Highly Targeted Named Accounts

You can also increase the chances of conversion by identifying very specific attributes for your ideal customer profile. For instance, you can hone in on companies that have experienced a real-world trigger (not online behavior) that would result in them being in-market, companies whose competitor activity is causing us to have an opportunity to steal share, or companies who have clear differentiation and sold social proof.

Thinking About Category

If someone is just thinking about the category of your solution, they still have a journey ahead of them before they're ready to meet with sales. These prospects still need to be nurtured in line with messaging developed collaboratively between marketing and sales.

Cold Audience

This audience is still a part of your ideal customer profile, but they are not thinking about the category and haven't had any particular triggers or engagement that would indicate they have buying intent. These should be the lowest on your priority list because these are going to be the hardest prospects to convert, at the highest cost.

Key Strategies in Sales Enablement

Once you know how to prioritize your efforts, how do you actually get started with effective sales enablement? Here are 6 key strategies to help salespeople prioritize and maximize every buyer interaction:

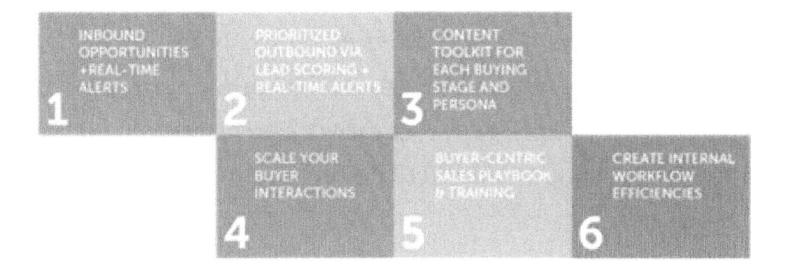

1 INBOUND OPPORTUNITIES +REAL-TIME ALERTS	2 PRIORITIZED OUTBOUND VIA LEAD SCORING + REAL-TIME ALERTS	3 CONTENT TOOLKIT FOR EACH BUYING STAGE AND PERSONA
4 SCALE YOUR BUYER INTERACTIONS	5 BUYER-CENTRIC SALES PLAYBOOK & TRAINING	6 CREATE INTERNAL WORKFLOW EFFICIENCIES

Inbound Opportunities + Real-Time Alerts: Yes, inbound is absolutely a sales enablement tactic. They close at 10-20x a cold call. They improve a salesperson's close rate and build up their talent for the next conversation.

Prioritized Outbound via Lead Scoring + Real-Time Alerts: Marketers can prioritize outbound efforts based on data and behavior, e.g. buyers who are demonstrating intent to purchase; and reach them with a relevant message based on their persona/behavior. Evan Carroll says "know something about them and use that to start the conversation."

Scaled Personalized Buyer Interactions: Salespeople are NOT being replaced. If anything, the world is moving back to an emphasis on personal relationships. We need to scale personalized communications to reach more people with a relevant message.

Content Toolkit for Each Buying Stage and Persona: Salespeople need to be able to readily access personalized content for every stage in the buyer journey for each persona.

So that their follow-ups/action steps continue to build trust and credibility – or assist in closing the deal when ready.

Buyer-Centric Sales Playbook & Training: Marketing should be in Sales' onboarding processes, and should have a key performance indicator, or KPI, around the amount of time to get to X revenue for a year 1 representative. The faster you can move a rep to "successful," the higher the retention and more revenue for the business.

Internal Workflow Efficiencies: It's critical to shadow the salespeople. After just one hour of observation, the findings on what marketing can provide in an automated way are astounding. Save them time to focus on the important work.

Strategies like these help your salespeople get their mojo back.

> Your
> sales
> people
> get thei
> mojo
> back.

When your salespeople feel supported, they can do better work and help your business grow. After implementing these strategies well, their experience will look something like this:

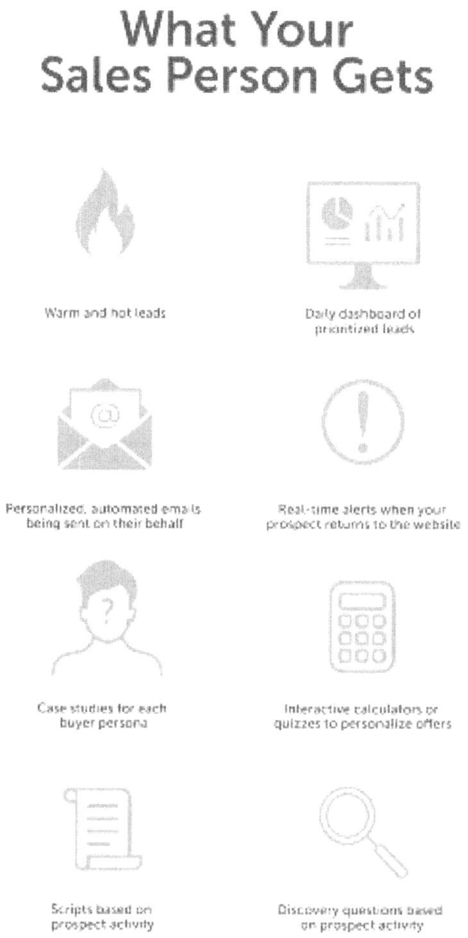

What Your Sales Person Gets

- Warm and hot leads
- Daily dashboard of prioritized leads
- Personalized, automated emails being sent on their behalf
- Real-time alerts when your prospect returns to the website
- Case studies for each buyer persona
- Interactive calculators or quizzes to personalize offers
- Scripts based on prospect activity
- Discovery questions based on prospect activity

Supporting Go-To-Market Strategy with Sales Enablement

Sales enablement strategies are essential to salespeople bringing your Go-To-Market strategy to life. A go-To-Market strategy is bigger than a marketing strategy. It's created within a strategic framework with data, customer interviews, and stakeholder discussions.

The Go-To-Market is defined with input from sales, marketing, product, finance, and IT. It maximizes everything the marketing team creates, by defining the business strategy in partnership with sales. Finally, all departments can row in the same direction.

A Go-To-Market strategy includes:

Positioning
How will you position in the market vs. competitors? Have you completed a win/loss analysis? What are the most profitable segments? Existing market share by segment? Are you creating a category or stealing share? What is the addressable universe & the best opportunity to win?

Segmentation
Who is your ideal customer profile (ICP), segments, and buyer personas?

Messaging
How will your messaging be buyer-centric and what content do you have to guide them along the buying journey?

Demand & Lead Generation
How are you reaching your ICP at the right time with the right message in the right place?

Marketing & Sales Technology
How will you leverage marketing and sales technology as the foundation to fuel success - Marketing Automation, CRM, CX, and other technology.

Value Proposition
What do you offer, including differentiation vs. your competitors? How does the buyer go through the purchase process and what are their purchase drivers?

Sales Enablement
How will you maximize each and every prospect - and increase close rate and average value?

Getting sales enablement right is key to executing a Go-To-Market strategy effectively. Sales enablement strategies can help you close any gaps in your strategy and get closer to reaching your business goals.

The first step is to see where those gaps are. Here are 7 statements to help guide your assessment of your Go-to-Market strategy, as well as how sales enablement can strengthen each area:

1. **We will easily turn away a new customer if there isn't a fit.**

Many companies reach for dollars with a short-term focus. It's understandable – it's hard to pass on an opportunity. However, even if you CAN do something, it doesn't mean you SHOULD.

When you can say NO, it means your strategy is tight. You know what you do and who you do it for, and that's incredibly special as you grow. That's how to grow margin through stronger close rates and more efficient business operations.

Another way to phrase this question could be: what portion of your business is in your sweet spot? This portion should be high if you want a healthy company set up for long-term growth.

How can a modern sales enablement approach help?

When a salesperson can say NO to a prospect offering to buy, you know that the company has a solid understanding of the importance of doing business with the right customers.

To get a sales rep to that point, they need to feel empowered and confident in the leads that are coming in from marketing, and the strategy that the team is pursuing. With strong alignment between sales and marketing and a collaborative approach to developing strategy, it'll be easier to give reps this confidence.

2. **Each member of sales and marketing can very clearly identify our target audience.**

Look at the business you've won over the last twelve months.

Does it look alike, and is there a similarity in what you're providing to each client? Does each client have similar firmographics like size or revenue? Are their needs similar?

If you can answer YES to all of those questions, that's great! If not, consider if you are trying to be everything to everyone. It would benefit you to hone in on your Go-To-Market strategy and define your target and value proposition. Even better, consider focusing solely on one niche, and then replicating from there.

In the book Scaling Up, Verne Harnish calls this "hyperspecialization." Margins and close rates go up because your entire existence is hyper-relevant to a niche group of prospects.

How can a modern sales enablement approach help?

If your sales team can't clearly identify your target audience, they need more support and clarity. It may not be all on them – if targeting and positioning decisions and updates aren't shared across the full team, then your reps won't be set up for success here.

Coming up with effective internal communication strategies, including meeting structure and resource repositories, is critical to empowering sales with the knowledge they need to be as effective as possible.

3. **We have a quarterly updated written strategy and action plan that rolls down across multiple departments, and those teams are collaborating at least monthly.**

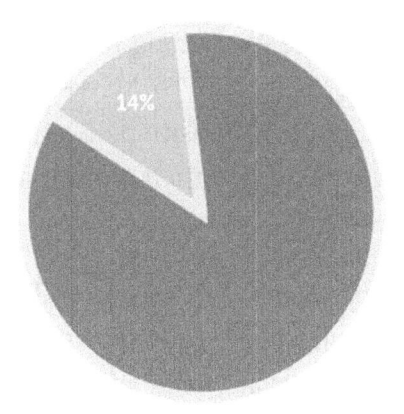

Only 14% of B2B organizations say they have an aligned planning process across product, marketing, and sales according to SiriusDecisions

14%

Only 14% of B2B organizations say they have an aligned planning process across product, marketing, and sales according to SiriusDecisions. Why?

- A lack of marketplace customer and competitive insights
- A lack of flexibility to validate the strategies with market feedback
- A lack of cross-department collaboration on creating the strategies
- A lack of focus, making the strategy far too broad, and making it difficult to take strategy to activation consistently across departments

Success all boils down to your people. Do you have the processes and frameworks to set them up for success? Is direction consistent and clear? Sales and marketing should be talking WEEKLY, if not more. This is where maximizing resources to commonly aligned goals is game-changing not only for results but also for culture.

How can a modern sales enablement approach help?

Part of sales enablement is making sure the sales team doesn't feel abandoned or stranded. With reps that are often off-site or in different time zones, it's not always easy to keep them in the loop with the goings-on in marketing, product, leadership, and other departments.

Strong internal communication and collaboration are incredibly important. Without the perspectives of all these different teams, your strategy will be disjointed or biased. With the sales team being the eyes and ears, having actual conversations with prospects, their point of view is invaluable and needs to be included when making strategic decisions.

4. **Each member of sales and marketing clearly articulates a value proposition and differentiation that has been validated against the market.**

This is an easy one to put to the test. Talk to employees, prospects you've won, prospects you've lost, and customers. Ask them, "What is the value of our offering? Why did you choose/not choose us?" Getting this data can help save you from wasting time on ineffective messages and strategies, and focus on what actually works.

How can a modern sales enablement approach help?

Circling back to effective internal communication – sales, marketing, and leadership need to be in lockstep with each other the whole way. When these teams work in tandem, you'll start to see significant results. Marketing understands what sales needs, sales can give marketing feedback on what might resonate in the field with prospects, and marketing can improve messaging and strategy. With regular collaboration, the teams' work feeds into each other and things run like a well-oiled machine.

5. **We have a strong lead generation – both quality and quantity – along with predictable sales revenue.**

If you have strong lead generation, consider what efficiencies you can gain in reducing customer acquisition costs. Get full closed-loop tracking that allows you to assess attribution and where you can push harder and where you can pull back.

How can a modern sales enablement approach help?

Even though marketing "does" lead generation, it'd be a mistake to think that sales don't also play a role. Sales are out in the field, talking to prospects and getting firsthand, honest reactions to the words, messages, and pain points that we think will resonate with the ideal client. Until these messages are validated with real people, our strategy isn't as sound as it could be.

When marketing and sales work together and have a healthy, communicative relationship, sales' experience in conversations with the prospects can inform the choices that marketing makes in new ads, content, web experience, and emails – which, in turn, will bring in a greater number of more highly qualified leads, enabling sales to do their jobs better and leading to greater success overall.

6. **We are leveraging sales and marketing technology to fuel our success – for example, customer relationship management (CRM), marketing automation, and other technology.**

It's astonishing how many companies pay for these tools and don't maximize them. If you're like most, you may only be fully utilizing 20% of the features and capabilities. Talk to colleagues, get on a call with the technology's support team, and follow marketing leaders to see what's possible. Do an audit to see which tools you can utilize better, which tools you're missing, and which tools you can unsubscribe from.

How can sales enablement help?

Tools can make a huge difference in a sales team's success. When you strip down barriers of tedious tasks, inefficient processes, and manual tracking, your sales team gets back more time in which they can focus on higher-impact tasks – like actually selling.

With the right automation and improved efficiencies, you can see increased capacity on your sales team; it's as if you'd hired another rep. Not only will efficiency skyrocket, but you'll have happier, less frustrated salespeople; which leads to better quality work and more closed deals.

7. **Our sales team contains strong performers that have a high retention rate.**

If you don't feel confident about this statement, it might not be the fault of your sales team. Today, sales are being asked to do more than really sets them up for success. They're stretched thin between cold outreach to prospects, working open opportunities, and sometimes, even managing existing customers – all without the proper tools and processes in place to help them prioritize leads and close deals more efficiently. Consider if you have a people, process, or system opportunity here.

How can sales enablement help?

The whole point of sales enablement is to increase the performance of your sales team. With better opportunities, help with prioritization, organized content management, and better efficiencies, you can build a sales team that performs and lasts.

Bonus: Take the Quiz! How strong is your Go-To-Market?

> Now let's put your Go-To-Market strategy to the test. Give yourself a rating between 1-5 on these seven statements (5 = strongly agree):

We will easily turn away a new customer if they're not a good fit for us.

1	2	3	4	5
☹	🙁	😐	🙂	😄

_____

Each member of sales and marketing can very clearly identify our target audience.

1	2	3	4	5
☹	🙁	😐	🙂	😄

_____

We have a quarterly, updated, written strategy and action plan that rolls down across multiple departments and those teams are collaborating at least monthly.

1	2	3	4	5
☹	🙁	😐	🙂	😄

_____

Each member of sales and marketing clearly articulates a value proposition and differentiation that has been validated against the market.

1   2   3   4   5   _____

We have strong lead generation – both quality and quantity – along with predictable sales revenue.

1   2   3   4   5   _____

We are leveraging sales and marketing technology to fuel our success – for example, CRM and marketing automation and other technology

1   2   3   4   5   _____

Our sales team contains strong performers that have a high retention rate

1   2   3   4   5   _____

TOTAL: _____

Check Your Results

31-35
Doing a good job

Your Go-To-Market strategy is strong! By bringing sales and marketing together, you're aligning messaging and strategy to create the best possible opportunities for growth.

21-30
On the right path

Your Go-To-Market strategy has some strengths, but there's still room to grow. Where do you see opportunities to better align your sales & marketing initiatives and develop a collaborative approach?

0-21
Needs work

Looks like your Go-To-Market strategy could use some help. Have you tried implementing modern sales enablement practices to align your teams and focus efforts to drive growth?

About Swivel

Swivel is a Cincinnati-based sales enablement company that helps B2B companies shift from brute-force to scalable growth with proven return on investment; or ROI.

B2B companies (10-500MM annual revenue) with highly considered purchases know the buyer landscape is changing, and are experiencing declining margins and unpredictable revenue. They know they need to upgrade to a modern method to accelerate growth, but they don't know-how. That's where we can help.

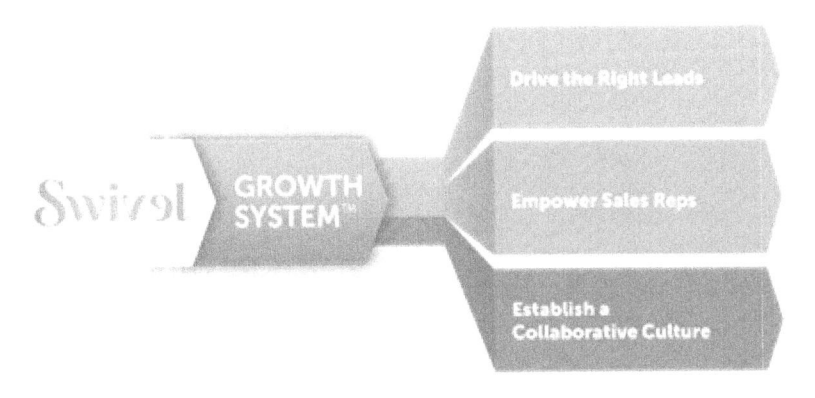

Swivel's approach focuses on 3 major initiatives encompassed in our modern approach to sales enablement. In this approach, we utilize Swivel's Growth System™ as a framework for each client that sets sales teams up for success and drives momentum toward predictable pipeline and business goals:

Drive the Right Leads

- The go-To-Market strategy that positions you with the best opportunity to win
- Content creation focused on attracting leads with buying intent
- A compelling buyer journey that drives leads down the funnel by meeting their needs wherever they are NOW

Empower Sales Reps

- Prioritize leads so reps are maximizing their time
- Streamline processes with tech to drive efficiency

- Support reps with content & strategy they need for the prospects they're talking to

Establish a Collaborative Culture

- Align sales & marketing to establish a culture that will drive a bigger impact on business goals over the long term
- Lead collaborative meetings to apply multiple perspectives to campaigns to better optimize and grow
- Build a repeatable, scalable system that's easy to replicate across additional product lines or audiences for future growth

We carry out these initiatives with Swivel's Growth System™ which maximizes 3 key factors:

1. **People**: You need 15+ skill sets to build an effective growth system. With Swivel, you have a CMO leading all of the flexible skill sets you need from month to month.

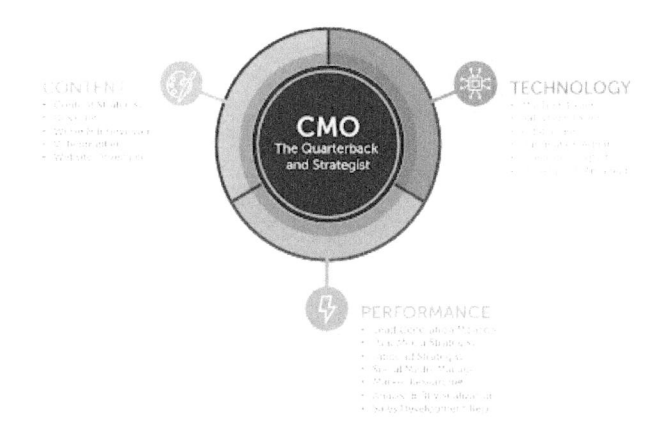

2. **Process**: Swivel builds customized growth strategies and systems that deliver leads that drive top-line revenue, sales

performance, and repeatable ROI.

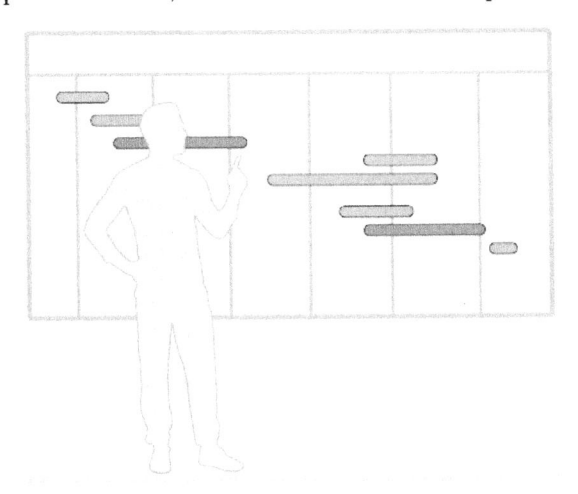

3. **Technology**: Swivel builds your tech stack. We automate as much as possible, integrate across systems, define data management, and establish a reporting strategy and cadence.

The Results

Through a collaborative approach between sales and marketing that maximizes and aligns every action with a strategic Go-To-Market, Swivel enables businesses to get predictable sales and achieve higher ROI from their efforts.

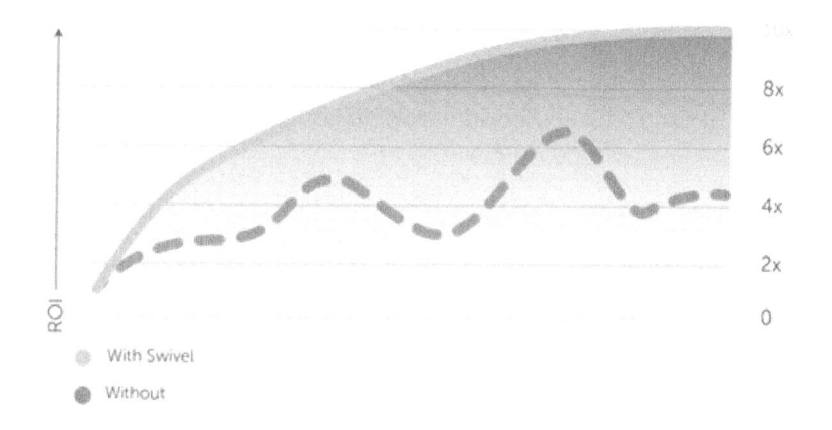

- Increased sales at higher margins
- Predictable, sustainable sales pipeline
- Increased close rate
- Reduced customer acquisition cost
- Maximize and retain your best salespeople

How to Get Started

Ready to see what other companies are doing to scale and better enable their sales teams? Get a FREE assessment of your sales enablement strategies today – go to www.swivelteam.com to schedule.

Notes

1. Skok, David. "Bridge Group 2015 Saas inside Sales Survey Report." For Entrepreneurs, Matrix Management Corporation, 27 Apr. 2016, https://www.forentrepreneurs.com/bridge-group-2015/.
2. "The Definitive Guide to Sales Enablement." Highspot, 4 Jan. 2022, https://www.highspot.com/sales-enablement/.

Simcha Kackley

"Many thanks for the development of this chapter go to Gracia Ostendorf, Swivel's Growth System Director; Addison Maly and Brian Kane, Swivel's Designers. I couldn't have done it without their support, ideas, and creativity." – Simcha Kackley

Simcha Kackley, Founder, and CEO of Swivel has held leadership Sales & Marketing roles in Cincinnati for 15+ years, including VP Marketing at The Business Backer, VP Sales and Marketing at IronRoad, and Director of Marketing at Champion Windows. Throughout her experience across various companies and marketing teams, she noticed one common pattern that was holding back businesses from success—placing the blame on sales reps for a lack of performance.

In 2018, Simcha founded her company, Swivel, with the intent of showing B2B businesses a better way to grow sales. Hiring salespeople for their Rolodex, pushing their way through linear growth, and then hiring new reps when those Rolodexes run out isn't a sustainable model. Instead, company leaders can get more from their existing sales team by maximizing their efforts with the right processes and standards in place, and with a better partnership between sales and marketing.

Swivel started helping companies like these go from brute force to scalable growth by empowering them with better lead generation, sales enablement, and sales development—all from one core, multi-disciplinary team. With a focus on collaboration and partnership between sales and marketing, Simcha developed the Growth System model for B2B sales success. The Growth System's emphasis on sales enablement allows companies to maximize their existing sales team, resulting in long-term, stable, predictable pipeline growth with increased close rates and higher margins. With wins in the technology, manufacturing, industrial, and services spaces, she has found that this approach brings success to a variety of companies in different industries.

Simcha has been an avid member of the local marketing and business scene in the Cincinnati area, acting as a board member and President of the Cincinnati chapter of the American Marketing Association for four and a half years, from 2012 to 2017. She's also passionate about giving back to the community, serving as a Big Sister in the Big Brothers Big Sisters of Greater Cincinnati since 2010. She was the Founder of the Rock n' Aspire Foundation, an annual Cincinnati-based fundraiser created to aspire music lovers to unify in support of the National MS Society, whose mission is to find a cure and address the challenges of everyone affected by MS. Here, she led the vision and creative development of the event concept, name, messaging, brand, website, email marketing, local marketing, and event marketing.

Simcha graduated with a BSBA in Marketing from Xavier University, as well as achieved an MBA with a marketing focus from the University of Cincinnati. She currently lives in Cincinnati with her husband, son, and 2 dogs, Riley and Chase.

CONNECT WITH SIMCHA KACKLEY:

https://www.linkedin.com/in/simcha/

Learn more about Simcha's company Swivel and its unique Growth System approach for small- and mid-market B2B businesses at www.swivelteam.com.

Conclusion

Thank you for supporting the Leadership Fusion authors by purchasing this book. The goal of this book is to help small to midsize business leaders with the tools, tactics, tips, and strategies to be the best leader for their company(ies). These thirteen authors have provided their expertise to the readers so that they can influence leadership in businesses beyond their own.

Being a strong leader looks different in every company. By understanding your business, your employees, and your business objectives and goals, you as the leader can step up to create an environment for success.

There were several themes in this book about leadership. Some key concepts were:

- Communication – communication includes speaking and listening. A strong leader can listen and understand the needs of the people and business and be able to communicate the goals and objectives of the business.
- Continuous Improvement – every leader starts with room for growth. Leaders must continue to change and adapt. Personal and professional development is a must for a strong leader.
- Connection – connect with your employees and build a professional relationship with them. Getting to know your employees and being able to provide them with the best

work environment is a top priority for a strong leader. Professional relationships are key here. Be sure to maintain that there is no favoritism or biases around your employees.

We hope you found a few good takeaways to implement from the book. We provide each author's bio and contact information so that you are able to connect with them. The authors are excited to help you achieve your leadership goals.

~Jodi Brandstetter

CEO, Influence Network Media

https://authors.influencenetworkmedia.com

https://linkedin.com/in/jodibrandstetter

About the Publisher:

Influence Network Media

We provide publishing & promotional services to business experts who want to become authors.

A media company that provides publishing and promotional coaching and services to authors who write non-fiction books around people in business. Founded by Jodi Brandstetter and Melanie Booher, Influence Network Media is a one-stop-shop to ensure your book is a bestseller and authors are able to use their book as a vessel to their career success.

Our offerings include:
- **Overnight Author** where in two days you are an author of one of our collective book series.
- **Collective Book** Opportunities where you only need one chapter, bio and headshot to become an Amazon Best Selling Author!
- **Solo Bundle** Opportunities for Business Experts who want to write a book that becomes a course and presentation all in one.
- **Micro Book** Opportunity for Business Experts that is less than 100 pages.

To learn more:
https://authors.influencenetworkmedia.com
Publishing@LETSCincy.com

Influence Network Media

Collaborative Book Series

Business Fusion

A Book Series Dedicated to Small to Midsize Businesses and their Success

Talent Fusion — Launched August 2021

Marketing Fusion — Launched January 2022

Leadership Fusion — Launched May 2022

Coming Soon:

Sales Fusion — Fall 2022

People Fusion — Winter 2023

Book Smarts Business Podcast

Short on time but big on growth? Then the Book Smarts Business Podcast is the podcast for you – the experienced, business professional who loves to listen to podcasts and read business books all in an effort to learn more about his/her profession, become an expert in their field, or maybe even become an entrepreneur down the road!

In 15 minutes, you will learn more about the expert authors, gain amazing insights and knowledge from their unique expertise, as well as the ins & outs about their book, and why they decided to write their book!

For a potential author, Book Smarts Business Podcast provides an avenue for business authors to showcase their expertise and book, and gain more readers for their book!

https://booksmartsbusiness.buzzsprout.com/

Made in the USA
Middletown, DE
03 June 2022